Also from Westphalia Press
westphaliapress.org

Saber & Scroll

Volume 1
Issue 1
Revised
April 2015

Editor-in-Chief,
Candace McGovern

WESTPHALIA PRESS
An imprint of Policy Studies Organization

Saber & Scroll: Volume 1, Issue 1, Revised April 2015
All Rights Reserved © 2019 by Policy Studies Organization

Westphalia Press
An imprint of Policy Studies Organization
1527 New Hampshire Ave., NW
Washington, D.C. 20036
info@ipsonet.org

ISBN-13: 978-1-63391-874-0
ISBN-10: 1-63391-874-2

Cover design by Jeffrey Barnes:
jbarnesbook.design

Daniel Gutierrez-Sandoval, Executive Director
PSO and Westphalia Press

Updated material and comments on this edition
can be found at the Westphalia Press website:
www.westphaliapress.org

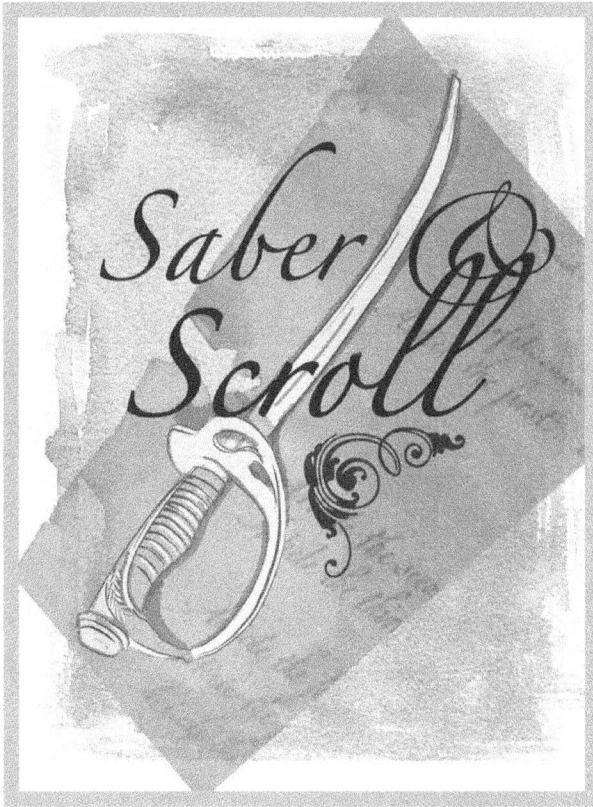

Saber and Scroll Journal

Volume I Issue I

Edited and Revised

April 2015

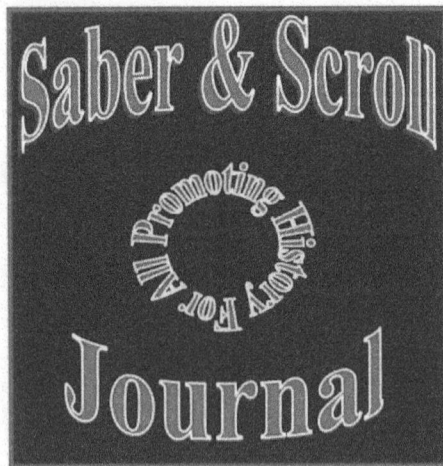

Contents

Letter from the Editor

Welcome to the edited and revised inaugural issue of the American Public University System (APUS) *Saber and Scroll Journal*. In the years since the APUS Saber and Scroll Historical Society launched its first journal issue, much has changed in the production of the journal. The journal team, working in partnership with APUS *e*Press, added a print-on-demand (POD) option for each issue in spring 2013. Authors of articles published in the earlier issues of the *Saber and Scroll* have expressed interest in purchasing a POD version of their work. In response to that request, a small team has tackled editing and revising the first issue of the journal to improve the content quality and publish it as a print offering.

Sincere thanks are due to APUS faculty member Jennifer Thompson, who, together with the *Saber and Scroll* Editor in Chief, have edited and revised each article and book review published in the first *Saber and Scroll* issue. Where appropriate, the team has added public domain artwork to feature articles to enhance the aesthetics of the issue. Thanks are also due to the inaugural issue authors: Jim Dick, Leigh-Anne Yacovelli, Kenneth Oziah, Lawrence Graves, Jennifer Thompson, Judy Monhollen, Alice Parker, Kathleen Mitchell Reitmayer, Anne Midgley, Shawn Ryan, and Candace McGovern.

The team wishes to express a special thanks to the first *Saber and Scroll* Editor in Chief, Candace McGovern, who shepherded the journal through unknown territory and launched what has become a successful history journal for APUS. Candaces's original Letter from the Editor is reproduced below:

I would like to begin by welcoming everyone to enjoy our inaugural edition of American Public University System's Saber and Scroll History Club and introducing myself as the new Editor-In-Chief. I graduated with an MA in Ancient and Classical History from American Public University and I am currently pursuing two graduate degrees, one in Humanities at APUS and an MA in Archaeology program at the University of Leicester. I have taught at a number of different museums in New York City and in San Diego. I have also taught at the High School and College level, primarily World Cultures and American History.

While my personal research focuses on everyday life in Ancient Greece and Rome including the roles of women and religion, this edition covers a wide range of topics and time periods from the American Civil War to the Battle of Nanking. I encourage all of our readers to enjoy topics outside their traditional scholarship and take advantage of an opportunity to explore what other new scholars in the field are researching. The goal of the *Saber and Scroll* journal is to foster intellectual growth and serve as a platform for students and other new researchers to share their ideas with others. Our focus will always be on students and those new to the field of historical scholarship. We invite our readers to submit letters and responses to papers featured in each edition and look forward to an exchange of scholarly ideas. I would also like to say a big thank you to the editorial staff, our advisor, club president and all those who helped to make this edition possible. With that, please enjoy our inaugural edition!

The team also expresses thanks to Kim Rush, the faculty advisor who expressed a Message from the Faculty with the inaugural issue:

My name is Kim Rush and I am the new faculty advisor for the Saber and Scroll. I started life out as a dancer and received a B.S. in Dance Management from Oklahoma City University, then I discovered I did not like working 18 hours days six to seven days a week, including holidays, so I turned to my next love – history. I received a master's degree in British history from Louisiana State University and am about a year away from receiving my Ph.D. in British history from LSU. My dissertation will look at the use of pageantry as propaganda at the court of Elizabeth I during the first decade of her reign.

I have been lucky enough to teach on the college level since I graduated from LSU the first time. I have taught for Southeastern Louisiana University, Colorado Technical University, and the University of Arkansas at Little Rock. I have taught for APUS since 2009. I mainly teach

American history courses and the research courses, but will start teaching European courses this year as well. My research interests are Tudor/Stuart Britain, the Renaissance, intellectual political history, and the early republic. I am also a contributing writer for Suite101.com and a reviewer for the Encyclopedia of Arkansas History. My first book, Historic Photos of Little Rock, was published in 2009.

I live outside Little Rock, Arkansas, with my husband and 14-month-old son. In my free time (ha!), I like to read, watch television and movies, play video games, and travel. I am looking forward to getting to know all of you better and please let me know if I can [help].

The first issue contained a segment, which the journal team has elected not to repeat in the later issues: Fun with History. Here are the items presented in that short-lived journal section.

If I could meet with any historian, I would choose Xenophon. Personally, I would start looking for him in any place which served wine, since it seemed he frequented those sorts of establishments. Once I found him, I would ask him all the usual questions of "Did it really happen?", "What was it like?", and so on. The primary reason I would choose Xenophon over other famous historians of the period stems from his writing style. He is one of my favorite historians of all time, with a good combination of entertainment and information. While his views on women leave a lot to be desired, particularly his idea a of a perfect wife, it seems like he would have been a fun guy to share a few glasses of wine with and have a nice conversation, but that could just be me.

Candace McGovern,
American Public University
University of Leicester

If I could go back in time and spend an afternoon with a historian of my choice, I think I would choose Herodotus. Widely known as the "Father of History," Herodotus wrote The Histories, which focused mainly on the Greco-Persian Wars. Greece in the time of Herodotus was an interesting place, before there was any union of the Greek city-states, and the Persians were a very dangerous threat. Born only four years after the death of Leonidas at the Battle of Thermopylae, he was able to give a unique history of that battle because it was still relatively fresh in the minds of the people. The Battle of Thermopylae has always fascinated me, and I would love to sit and talk about theories behind the strategy with Herodotus.

Judy Monhollen,
American Public University

With apologies to the fine writers of the BBC series, *Doctor Who,* the following is an alternate ending to *The Girl in the Fireplace* episode: Jeanne-Antionette "Reinette" Poisson, Madame du Pompadour, clutched the Doctor's sleeve as they ducked through the fireplace in her bed-chamber to arrive on the deck of an abandoned fifty-first century space ship, the *Madame du Pompadour.* The Doctor had promised to take her anywhere she desired in time and space, and Reinette immediately made her wish known; to visit Herodotus. "He has been my inspiration for many years, and I wish to speak to him." Slipping into the TARDIS, they set the controls for Greece, circa 450 B.C.E. Reaching their destination, they sought out Herodotus. The Doctor introduced Reinette to his old friend, since, of course, this was not his first visit to Pericles' Athens. Herodotus was only too pleased to expound on his philosophy of history and learning. History provides examples of the use and abuse of power; "Is it not the duty of all to understand from whence they came to better design the path ahead," he asked? She nodded in agreement with all he said, and asked that he acquaint her with his favorite story. "Ah, the tale of the Spartans' courage and sacrifice at Thermopylae," he began, launching into a tale of the doomed three hundred. As the sun began to sink, the Doctor interrupted the dialogue. "I hear that great statesmen and military leaders are pushed from the center stage of history in twentieth century historiography, replaced by commoners." Both looked at him disbelievingly, shook their heads in amusement at such a preposterous thought, and continued discussing Thermopylae.

Anne Midgley

It is with great pleasure then that the edited and revised version of the Saber and Scroll inaugural issue is hereby presented in print-on-demand format.

Anne Midgley
Editor in Chief

Saratoga: The Turning Point of the American Revolution

Jim Dick

The American Revolution was more than just a civil war between the rebels in Great Britain's North American colonies along the Atlantic seaboard and Great Britain. The conflict eventually escalated into a vast worldwide war between Great Britain and her traditional adversaries, France, Spain, and the Netherlands who allied with the American rebels. While no country aided the American rebel colonists at first, their victory in the Saratoga campaign resulted in a shift to recognition by Britain's continental foes who saw an opportunity to capture territory of their own and humble the arrogance of Great Britain. The loss of a British army in the Saratoga campaign was the decisive factor which caused France to enter the American Revolution, thus transforming the conflict from a civil war to an international war, which was the only way the colonies were able to gain their independence.

As armed rebellion began between Great Britain and the American rebels in 1775, it was apparent that the British vastly outgunned the Americans. Fortunately, the French did surreptitiously send arms to the Americans early in 1777, replacing much of the losses incurred during the 1776 campaign season.[1] Still, the Americans were chronically short of artillery power as they would be throughout the war. The campaign season of 1776 had resulted in the capture of New York City and the entire colony of New Jersey. The British had driven General George Washington, commander of the Continental Army, completely across the Delaware River by the end of 1776. Only a daring raid launched on Christmas evening that resulted in the capture of the British garrisons of Princeton and Trenton in late December salvaged any hope of victory for the Americans.

As the campaign season of 1777 dawned, General Washington had two problems. He knew the British were sending a force from Canada under General John Burgoyne whose mission was to drive south, take Fort Ticonderoga, and meet General William Howe's force in Albany. Washington's army could not move north unless Howe's army moved from New York City; otherwise, Pennsylvania would be vulnerable to an invading British force under Howe. The state of Washington's army was such that he had to avoid a decisive battle with the British as it would favor the British Army overwhelmingly.

This left an army under the command of General Horatio Gates to defend the northern area against General Burgoyne's southward driving British force. Everyone on both sides expected Howe to drive north along the Hudson River to link up with Burgoyne's army which would effectively cut New England off from the rest of the colonies. Instead, Howe led his army out in an attempt to force a decisive battle with Washington's Continentals and took Philadelphia, the rebel capital. Burgoyne's force was left on its own to smash Gates' army.

General John Burgoyne, commander of the British force coming south from Canada, was an aggressive officer. At the same time, he was the typical product of the British officer corps. He liked his luxuries even on campaign. To this end, he brought his mistress and thirty carts of personal goods on the campaign despite the desperate need of the wagons to haul military supplies his army needed.[2] Burgoyne was a legendary gambler as well. His campaign would be no different. He made his plans with the Secretary of State for the Colonies, Lord George Germain, a man the British Army had cashiered in 1759 and who had won his post through political means.[3] Between these two men, they planned a campaign that failed to take into account many factors which most British commanders would continue to ignore throughout the entire war.

Burgoyne's first mistake was his failure to understand the terrain and the challenges it would present to his campaign. The sheer size of the colonies repeatedly frustrated the British in the war as military planners in London failed to comprehend the distances involved. Mistaken assumptions about the campaign distance left Burgoyne with a supply chain stretched out over miles; he was simply unable to defend it. The second flaw was overestimating the number of British Loyalists, or Tories, that would join and support Burgoyne's invasion force. During the war, Lord Germain continually imagined Loyalists everywhere in the colonies, but they often failed to materialize.[4] The third flaw in the campaign was in splitting Burgoyne's forces into two separate commands and expecting them to accomplish their objectives, and then to link up on the Hudson River.

This second force, led by Lieutenant Colonel Barry St. Leger, was too small and depended too heavily upon expected Tories and Mohawk Indians to achieve its goals. While Burgoyne went south along the Lake Champlain route, St. Leger was supposed to sail across Lake Ontario and then strike east, take the dilapidated ruin of old Fort Stanwix, and drive along the Mohawk River valley to the Hudson River. Instead, St. Leger and his force suffered a loss in a fierce battle at Oriskany which discouraged his fickle Mohawk allies who had expected an easy fight.[5] St. Leger's force would fail to achieve any of its goals and never recovered from the almost complete defection of the Mohawks once they were fed disinformation by a trick of the American General Benedict Arnold. Arnold sent a condemned crazy man into the British camp with a wild story about numerous Americans preparing to attack the British.

This trick played upon the Mohawk's respect for insane people who they thought were touched by the gods. They never doubted the babbling man, Han Yost, or his story of 3,000 Americans led by Arnold that were about to attack them.[6] The Mohawks panicked and fled, ransacking the camp as they left. The British and Tories followed them as well. Arnold was able to capture St. Leger's supplies and cannon ending the threat from the west.

Burgoyne and Howe were unaware of this development. As it was, Burgoyne won a major victory at Fort Ticonderoga without a fight. The French had constructed this fort prior to the Seven Years' War. Its original purpose was to guard against an invasion force going into Canada. The British had allowed the fort to fall into disrepair, and Benedict Arnold and Ethan Allen's Green Mountain Boys seized the fort early in the war. It was supposed that with the repairs to the fort, it would guard against an invasion force coming from Canada. Instead, the fort's commander realized that the fort was wide open to a bombardment from a nearby hill. Unable to defend the fort and the hill with the troops he had, the American commander abandoned the fort when Burgoyne's army arrived.[7]

Fortunately for the Americans, the terrain between Fort Ticonderoga and the Hudson River was a wilderness with few roads. What roads and bridges there were, General Gates had woodsmen destroy. General Horatio Gates was a former British officer who had two advantages over Burgoyne that he used to great effect. One was that he knew Burgoyne's character as a gambler and anticipated that Burgoyne would continually gamble on victory despite any setbacks.[8] The second advantage lay in the elongated supply lines of the British. Burgoyne would not be able to reestablish them if they were cut. In this case, the battle suited Gates who assumed a defensive nature and waited for Burgoyne's army to arrive.

One of the biggest blunders of the British during the war helped the American effort. Instead of sending his army, or at least a significant force up the

Hudson River to link up with Burgoyne, General Howe decided to attack and capture Philadelphia. Once Howe boarded his troops and ships in July of 1777 and sailed to the Delaware River to attack Pennsylvania and Philadelphia, Washington was free to deploy the American forces accordingly.[9] This allowed American militia troops from New England to support Gates and the Northern Command since Howe's forces were committed in Pennsylvania. Burgoyne and his invasion force would be unsupported, although Burgoyne still thought Howe would send a force to Albany when Burgoyne's army approached the town.

After Burgoyne reached the Hudson, the real fighting began. Baron Friedrich von Riedesel led the Hessians, who composed part of the British force. His wife, Baroness Frederika von Riedesel, accompanied the invasion force as it made its way south. Her journal gave an excellent account of the day-to-day life in the British camp as well as an observation of General Burgoyne himself. According to the Baroness, the general spent a great deal of his time with his mistress and their champagne.[10] Burgoyne's delays kept consuming his supplies and once the fighting started, he ran through them quickly.

Burgoyne's army fought its first major battle at Bennington. They sent a foraging party of Hessians to capture much needed horses and a rumored Continental powder magazine there. Instead, this foraging party ran into General John Stark and his New Hampshire militia who delivered a crushing defeat to the Hessians. Another Hessian force they sent in relief met the same fate. Only darkness enabled some of the Hessian force to escape. That battle cost Burgoyne over one thousand men dead or captured by the Americans, and gave the American militia a much needed victory. The Saratoga campaign was one of the few times when the American militia fought extremely well during the Revolution. In this instance, they were fighting on their own ground with their own leader; often not the case.

Following Bennington, Burgoyne's main body continued onward trying to close with the American army and force battle. Gates refused to fight until he could gain an edge over the British. Instead, he sent out the sharpshooting riflemen of General Daniel Morgan's Virginia Regiment to harass the British. Daily, the British continued to lose men to these unorthodox tactics. Finally, they fought Battle of Freeman's Farm on September 19. Morgan's riflemen took a deadly toll of British officers and artillerymen. The battle seesawed back and forth across the field throughout the day. By nightfall the Americans fell back, but the British had clearly lost the battle. They lost over six hundred irreplaceable men while the Americans had only sixty-five known dead.[11]

The balance of forces had drastically swung in the Americans' favor. Militiamen poured into the American camp while Burgoyne's unreliable Indian allies deserted him. The situation had grown grim for the British. The British troops in New York City, over seven thousand of them, made one raid up the Hudson River, but their timid commander, General Sir Henry Clinton, was too fearful of a possible flank attack by American troops and refused to drive further north, thus leaving Burgoyne's army to their fate.[12]

On October 7, Burgoyne moved to attack. Outnumbered, the British fought valiantly under one of their best generals, Simon Fraser, until Arnold and Morgan ordered him deliberately shot. Once Fraser fell, the British line began to crumble. Arnold, who Gates had been relieved of command earlier in the day, disobeyed orders and dashed about furiously on the battlefield committing and exhorting the American regiments to victory. Wounded in the leg, Arnold's bravery carried the day for the Americans who completely routed the British.[13] With this loss, the British had lost over half of their invasion force.

Burgoyne also had supply difficulties which had been ignored in his erstwhile gamble on victory. He simply did not have enough cartage to carry a large amount of critical supplies. That left him dependent on a consistent supply route which the Americans cut off following the second Saratoga battle; the Battle of Bemis Heights. His army was still capable of

Figure 1 *Surrender of General Burgoyne.* Oil on canvas by John Trumbull, 1821. Rotunda, US Capital.

fighting its way back to Fort Ticonderoga, and General Riedesel and the other British generals prepared to do so. Instead, Burgoyne inexplicably halted the retreat to entertain himself at the mansion of the former American commander, General Philip Schuyler.[15]

While he delayed, the American militia continued to pour into the area until the British were outnumbered three to one.

Following a British council of war, Burgoyne vacillated hoping that some relief from the south would come, but none materialized. Finally he agreed to surrender his army to the Americans on October 17, 1777. Even with this victory, the Continental Army faced major problems. General Gates refused to send regiments loaned to his command by General Washington back to Pennsylvania where they were desperately needed.[16] Instead, he did not even bother to notify his commander, but instead directly reported to Congress on his victory.[17]

The Conway Cabal against Washington would later implicate Gates. Washington and the Continental Army, who Howe's force had brushed aside as it took Philadelphia at the Battle of Brandywine, counterattacked and fought a dynamic battle against the British at Germantown, actually driving the British from the battlefield before a series of mistakes and communication breakdowns caused the Americans to retreat.[18] One German officer present at the battle exclaimed that he had just seen, "something I have never seen before, namely the English in full flight."[19]

This battle, significant to many European military observers as displaying great promise for the Continental Army, was coupled with the amazing American victory at Saratoga by the American ambassador to the French court in Versailles, Benjamin Franklin. Even before the Declaration of Independence, the Continental Congress had secretly created a Committee of Correspondence. Its mission was to seek out foreign aid and support.[20] To that end, they dispatched Silas Deane, the first American representative to France. Humiliated by the losses of the Seven Year's War, France, had a foreign minister, the Comte de Vergennes, who wanted to strike back at the British. The French aided the Americans quietly, even allowing American privateers to use French ports, which stretched the Royal Navy into an Atlantic wide sea war it was not prepared to fight.[21]

Once the news of Saratoga reached Benjamin Franklin, he used it as evidence, along with the daring attack by Washington at Germantown, that the United States could win the Revolution. He also dangled the Carlisle Commission, a British attempt at a negotiated settlement with the Americans, as more proof that the British could lose the war.[22] The French fears of an Anglo-American reconciliation led the French into signing a treaty of alliance with the United States in February, 1778. The American Revolution, which had started out as a civil war between the Thirteen Colonies in North America versus their overlord,

Great Britain, had become a worldwide war which then threatened Great Britain and its colonies across the globe. When Spain and the Netherlands entered the conflict the following year, British forces were stretched too thin.

As a result, when a combined French and American army and naval blockade forced the surrender of General Charles Earl Cornwallis's army at Yorktown in 1781, the British realized they had lost the conflict. Peace was negotiated in 1783. Before Saratoga, the American rebels were barely hanging onto their newly declared freedom, suffering two years of almost complete defeats and the losses of both New York City and Philadelphia. After Saratoga, the Americans were able to secure foreign allies and expand the conflict beyond North America. The Saratoga campaign, ill planned and ill executed by the primary British commanders involved, turned out to be the strategic victory that ultimately secured the independence of the United States of America in the American Revolution.

Notes

1. John S. Pancake, *1777: The Year of the Hangman* (Tuscaloosa: University of Alabama Press, 1977), 79.

2. Fred J. Cook, *Dawn Over Saratoga* (Garden City: Doubleday & Company, 1973), 5.

3. John R. Elting, *The Battles of Saratoga* (Monmouth Beach: Philip Freneau Press, 1977), 14.

4. Ibid., 21.

5. Ibid., 38.

6. Cook, *Dawn Over Saratoga,* 87.

7. John Ferling, *Almost a Miracle: The American Victory in the War of Independence* (Oxford: Oxford University Press, 2007), 220.

8. Cook, *Dawn Over Saratoga,* 6.

9. General George Washington, "Washington's General Orders, September 5, 1777," *The American Revolution, 1763-1783,* http://www.loc.gov (accessed July 17, 2010).

10. Baroness Frederika von Riedesel, *Baroness von Riedesel and the American Revolution: Journal and Correspondence of a Tour of Duty, 1776-1783,* trans. Marvin L. Brown (Chapel Hill: University of North Carolina Press, 1965).

11. Cook, *Dawn Over Saratoga,* 132.

12. Cook, *Dawn Over Saratoga,* 152.

13. Elting, *Battles of Saratoga,* 62.

14. Pancake, *The Year of the Hangman,* 189.

15. Cook, Dawn Over Saratoga, 175.

16. General George Washington, "George Washington to Horatio Gates, October 30, 1777," *The American Revolution, 1763-1783*, http://www.loc.gov (accessed July 19, 2010).

17. James Flexner, *Washington: The Indispensable Man* (New York: Back Bay Books, 1969), 109.

18. Ibid., 106.

19. Robert K. Wright, Jr., *The Continental Army* (Washington D.C.: Center of Military History, 1983), 118.

20. Pancake, *Year of the Hangman,* 214.

21. Ibid., *215.*

22. Gordon S. Wood, *The American Revolution* (New York: Modern Library, 2002), 82.

BIBLIOGRAPHY

Cook, Fred J. *Dawn over Saratoga: The Turning Point of the Revolutionary War.* Garden City: Doubleday & Company, 1973.

Elting, John R. *The Battles of Saratoga.* Monmouth Beach: Philip Freneau Press, 1977.

Ferling, John. *Almost a Miracle: The American Victory in the War of Independence.* New York: Oxford University Press, 2007.

Flexner, James Thomas. *Washington: The Indispensable Man.* New York: Back Bay Books, 1969.

Pancake, John S. *1777: The Year of the Hangman.* Tuscaloosa: The University of Alabama Press, 1977.

Riedesel, Baroness Frederika von. *Baroness von Riedesel and the American Revolution: Journal and Correspondence of a Tour of Duty, 1776-1783.* Translated by Marvin L. Brown. Chapel Hill: University of North Carolina Press, 1965.

Washington, General George. "George Washington to Horatio Gates, October 30, 1777." *The American Revolution, 1763-1783,* http://www.loc.gov (accessed July 19, 2010).

_____. "Washington's General Orders, September 5, 1777." *The American Revolution, 1763-1783.* http://www.loc.gov (accessed July 17, 2010).

Wood, Gordon S. *The American Revolution.* New York: Modern Library, 2002.

Wright, Jr., Robert K. *The Continental Army.* Washington D.C.: Center of Military History, United States Army, 1983.

Who Got Stuck with the Bill?

Introduction

The Federalists' plan to reduce the new nation's debt resulted in several crises, one of which was the Whiskey Rebellion. The events that unfolded in western Pennsylvania could have happened along any of the frontier areas. Virginia and Tennessee both felt the effects of the whiskey tax, but Pennsylvania, with its system of government that was the closest to true democracy, seemed to draw the most attention from government leaders. The residents of western Pennsylvania fought for the acknowledgement of their needs by the leaders in the eastern part of the state. Specifically, the "Whiskey Boys," some of the men from Pennsylvania's western half, fought for the repeal of a law that mostly affected the people along the frontier border. These same men became the focus of the federal government's attention as it implemented its plan to unburden the new nation from its national debt. This move by the government caused the division between Republicans and Federalists to widen, and established the executive branch's right to use the military to quell domestic upheaval.

A Challenged Nation

After gaining their independence from England, and since neither English law nor their charters, if applicable, applied to them any longer, many of the former colonies created constitutions to reflect their new status. Rhode Island was an exception; it did not retire its charter and adopt a new constitution until 1843. Pennsylvania's constitution provided for government by a Quaker oligarchy. Revolutionary War leaders sided with democratic leaders rather than Quaker leaders because of their loyalist leanings. Thus, the new constitution created a more true democratic government. No longer did only a few religious leaders have the power to decide the laws governing Pennsylvania. Neither was this right held only to landowners as seen in other states with Federalist leanings. Instead, everyone had a voice, even the westerners, to the dismay of those in the East. Voters in the West usually did not make the polls because of distance and terrain, but if they did, the new person in the Assembly was one who lived in the West, not just owned land there. Examples of this were Robert Whitehall, a farmer, and William Findley, a weaver,[1] men known and trusted by their neighbors whose politics was similar to theirs. This new legislature passed laws that favored small farmers rather than large companies that held a monopoly on goods.

The "bad blood" between the wealthy landowners in the East and the poorer people who lived along the western frontier dates back before the Revolutionary War. The early 1770s saw the occurrence of the War of Regulation. Farmers and artisans in North Carolina, tired of the corrupt political dealings of their leaders, managed to shut down their local governments in an attempt to elicit change. They viewed their leaders as concerned with only the eastern merchants and lawyers holding office, who passed laws against the farmers in West. The Regulators attacked the courts to draw attention to their plight. However, the governor used the garrisoned troops to quell the insurrections. Not only was the War of Regulation significant in highlighting governmental rivalry between East and West, but a leader of the Whiskey Rebellion, Herman Husband, took part in the North Carolina attacks before he fled to Pennsylvania.[2]

As time wore on, it became obvious that the Articles of Confederation were not adequate to address the growing debt to foreign countries and its veterans. Arising out of the distress caused by the Articles was an insurrection tied closely to the Whiskey Rebellion: Shays' Rebellion. From 1786 to 1787, Massachusetts farmers pled with their government officials for debt relief. Many of the small farmers were not able to pay the mortgages on their land, or only had worthless paper money while their creditors required payment in gold or silver. They issued petitions and held protests, but their government officials only passed more laws that seemed to make things worse. Daniel Shays gathered over a hundred armed men and marched on Boston when the courts charged eleven former Revolutionary War veterans with rioting after they and some of their neighbors tried to shut down the government. Boston's elite saw Daniel Shays and his followers as disputing their control, and called in the militia to bring them to justice.

After the approval of the Constitution, the debt of the individual states to foreign countries became the nation's debt, and Alexander Hamilton pushed through excises on luxury items such as whiskey to pay for it, which affected the citizens living in the frontier sections of the states more than the people who lived along the East coast. Revenue from the excise was lower in some states than the cost of collection, as was the case in Georgia, because only the coastal areas saw enforcement. In Kentucky, the law was a "dead letter."[3] Places like Northwest Virginia, and the western sections of North and South Carolina were the same as Kentucky.

Petitions asking for the repeal of the whiskey tax came from Pennsylvania, Virginia, North Carolina, and Maryland's legislatures. The government's answer to their protests was the removal of the right of local courts to indict citizens with tax evasion. This added to the problems for the farmers in western Pennsylvania because they now had to attend trial in Philadelphia, over three hundred miles from home, and often during their busiest farming season, which kept them from making money to pay for necessities and their land, and which led to foreclosure. Thus, the people in the West viewed it as deliberate confiscation of land by Easterners.[4] Speculators from the eastern cities purchased the foreclosed land in the West.

The History and Purpose of Whiskey Taxes

The excise on whiskey in 1791 was not the first time a government taxed this item. Whiskey taxes existed from 1684-1791, sometimes to provide money for fighting the French, other times to pay bills of credit. There was no regular collection of taxes due to the irregular passage of laws, and the unpopularity of the tax. Whiskey was a constant target for taxes because of its wide array of uses from people of all lifestyles. Those who lived the frontier's hard lifestyle found whiskey an easy and accessible luxury. It also held great importance in medicine because of its use for fevers, snakebites, and pain. The army even gave it to its soldiers with their rations. For a while, rum from the Caribbean was cheaper than distilling wheat and rye, but this only lasted until the non-importation laws went into effect. The surge in demand for locally distilled alcohol created a shortage of bread. In order to regulate the stills, Congress instituted a law in 1778 that forbade distilling for part of the year, but the government eventually saw no further use for it, and repealed it.[5]

There was always the view that taxes like the whiskey tax were the reason why the Americans went to war against England. A more specific argument used by the Republicans was that taxes on whiskey made it too expensive to make because it was a tax on production, not sales. The Federalists said it was a tax on the wealthy, who bought distilled liquor. A game of semantics ensued between party leaders when the Republicans countered this argument, and pointed out that the wealthy did not pay the tax because their whiskey was stored in large casks.

The whiskey tax also affected the small farmer in the West more than those in the East because they did not have the access to coin money the way the Easterners did. Small western farmers and immigrants bartered with whiskey and produce to purchase what they needed from area merchants, as well as the army for the cash needed to pay for their land. The whiskey tax left no money for any items other than necessities, which further highlighted the Westerners' lack of access to markets, and that the eastern elitists owned their land.

Farmers brought whiskey over the Alleghenies by horse in large casks called kegs. A horse could hold two kegs, each holding six to eight gallons; whereas a horse could only carry four bushels of rye grain. The demand for this grain was not high enough for the grower to see a profit. However, the people wanted whiskey, so the farmer made rye whiskey from the unwanted grain. In 1794, the army paid almost fifty cents per gallon whiskey, but only forty cents per bushel rye.[6] For transportation purposes, this meant a horse could carry more earning capacity if it carried whiskey. To keep the trip cost effective, distillers usually sent twenty to thirty horses at one time to eastern markets. By 1793, the Ohio River to the Mississippi saw nearly one-third of these caravans, but because Spain closed the Mississippi to travel, overland essentially became the only way to market.[7]

Another benefit the wealthy Easterners had at their disposal was the availability of large stills. Western neighbors went in together on a distillery because a good one, a one hundred gallon still, cost as much as a two hundred acre farm. These farmers used the shared still similar to a shared mill. They paid for their share of the still out of their whiskey supply since the one whose property it sat on usually paid up front for the still. Hamilton said it was the distiller's fault for not making the customer pay the production tax. Stills in the East had customers at the site of production, and could pay their tax immediately. The stills in the West could be as large as those stills in the East, but the whiskey had to make it to market. The Westerners had to wait for the sale, and since the whiskey tax was on the size of the still, there was the ongoing problem of transportation, and customers in the East still demanded the same low price for whiskey, there was no room for profit anymore. No profit meant the West became the greatest consumer of its whiskey. No matter what, they still had to pay the tax.

The tax schedules for a city, town, or village were nine to twenty-five cents per gallon by proof, and if a distiller could pay quarterly, they received discounts. The tax code charged country distillers sixty cents per gallon for still capacity, or nine cents per gallon for production. A later act in 1792 reduced the rates. If a still was less than four hundred gallons, it cost fifty-four cents per gallon annually, ten cents per gallon per month in use, or seven cents per gallon produced. Further amending the act was the Act of 1794, which allowed stills of one hundred gallons or less to pay the monthly fee annually.[8]

Opinions and Feelings

Pennsylvania's people were no different from other states, and Pennsylvania's population saw a distinct division into two sections created by wealth. The first group contained the old money landowners, merchants, and manufacturer owners, who were proud of their heritage and birth. As the United States expanded, the second set of people continued to increase, small farmers, artisans, and new immigrants, all of whom were proud of being equal. This growing sector of the population settled in the West because the existing people already owned and operated everything for their own profit in the East, leaving no room for newcomers. The Westerners said the reasons for their rebellion were simply from a hatred of taxes, riding the tide of the popular anti-tax movement from the Revolutionary War, and from the abundance of Scotch-Irish people who now lived in the area. These Scotch-Irish immigrants came to America harboring a tremendous hatred of the tax collector, and were the biggest instigators of the Whiskey Rebellion.[9]

The Whiskey Rebellion was essentially a regional rebellion. Because the United States still had a decentralized federal government, as the Constitution was relatively new, the local governments continued to take charge of situations that arose. These people were also the ones responsible for the collection of taxes. However, they did not support or enforce taxes because they benefitted from positions of power. That is, until the federal government forced them to abide by their positions under the threat of removal of their authority.[10] These leaders used the Scotch-Irish's natural hatred of the tax collector, and the popular sentiment regarding taxes in general, and incited the public. They later claimed they were part of the rioting to calm down the distillers who terrorized tax collectors.[11]

There were three groups involved in the events that led to the Whiskey Rebellion. The first group contained the elite economic and political leaders of the West, the distillers. Since the whiskey tax affected them directly, they swayed the protests. The area's elected and appointed leaders were the ones who gathered in Pittsburgh for the meetings in September 1791 and August 1792, which led to the resolution that so incited President Washington. The militiamen formed the second group. These military-minded men could reprimand the tax collector, and through their actions, they supported protesters.[12] Ultimately, the reason for the rebellion was the third and largest group, the general public. The leaders took their cue from the public, who felt they still had a right to demand a choice and have a say in the governing.

West Versus East

The commoners in the West knew about important events before their mail arrived. Politics moved with the wagon trains that crossed the state carrying whiskey and furs. These people were not stupid, as is so often believed. Even graduates of Princeton found themselves in western Pennsylvania for a chance to make it big. People like Hugh Brackenridge, a western lawyer and a leader of the rebellion, did not have the opportunity to become rich and famous in the East. The West offered this chance. The major religions for those who lived in the western frontier, the Presbyterians and Episcopalians, required their religious leaders to hold an education. The common people also demanded and built academies for their children to attend. The literacy rate in western Pennsylvania was sixty-five percent. This was impressive given that England's was sixty percent, and France's was only fifty percent.[13]

Easterners called the people who lived in western Pennsylvania stupid because many only had the minimal creature comforts, such as homespun clothes, and wooden dishes, not china. Instead of multicourse meals with a variety of ingredients brought in through coastal trade similar to what the Easterners had, the people in the western counties ate corn meal, pork, game, some vegetables, and wild berries. The townsfolk and gentlemen farmers had as much as their cohorts in the East, but the East saw the Westerners as all the same.

The East had a definite hierarchy of landlords and tenants, and wanted to keep its power. After all, they postured, the federal government was there, and they were the oldest settlements. This feeling of entitlement was the cover speculators used. The West disliked the idea of the assumption of war debts by the government, because it was mostly speculator money. Moreover, the West believed that the people who held the bonds had done nothing to deserve payment.[14] Many farmers faced foreclosure on land, and prison for taxes, because the wealthy speculators in the East bought the foreclosed land in West. This supported the Westerners' view that Easterners were greedy. The small farmers could not get loans from the state's bank, only speculators with access to gold and silver coin could, which resulted in more foreclosures. Pennsylvania's legislature had Westerners in the Assembly, who forced the revocation of the bank's charter, and refused to charter it again the next session. However, the purchase of bonds to pay state debt was popular even among the lesser rich, so speculation continued.

Westerners viewed themselves as part of a perfect democracy, and demanded the government leave the farmers, artisans, and laborers alone, and regulate the lawyers, bankers, and large landowners. Westerners wanted a land tax because of eastern speculators who owed mortgages on most of the western lands, which is where the extra cash of farmers went. The whiskey tax, said the Westerners, was simply eastern money ruling the government.[15] The Easterners accused those in the West of not pulling their weight in sharing the expense of paying the government's debt. What many Easterners failed to realize was that the Westerners were usually among the first to pay their taxes.[16] That is, except the whiskey tax.

The Insurrection

Post-Revolutionary War, the people who lived in western Pennsylvania avoided foreclosures and tax collectors by crowd activities, which threatened local agents into not doing anything. They blocked roads with items such as fences and logs to keep judges and jurors from attending courts. Witnesses who testified against tax evaders saw their barns burned, and distillers who paid their tax found themselves tarred and feathered, and their stills destroyed. Men dressed as Indians, women, and black-faced vigilantes tarred and feathered tax collectors, another common occurrence. Likewise, landlords, who rented office space to the tax collectors, saw their buildings destroyed. It was unfortunate, but the law required the posting of the Offices of Inspection so people knew where to go to pay their tax.

This gave Tom the Tinker enough time to cause problems for the owners of the building.

Tom the Tinker became a people's favorite for advertising the latest offenders so the public could act against them. During one riot, James Kiddoe had his still shot full of holes. John Holcroft, the leader of the rioters, laughed and said Tom was tinkering with the still. This gave rise to the infamous name. It became Tom's job to shut down the Offices of Inspection so that there was no compliance with law. Anyone could play the role of Tom the Tinker, and everyone took part in protesting the tax. Even prominent, wealthy landowners in the West shared in the protest when they published tax records in the papers, and petitions of aggrieved parties.

People knew there were other troubled spots in the United States, but the Federalists were too good with publicity, and made it seem as if ending the resistance in Pennsylvania would end all the problems. Hamilton wrote in the *Gazette of the United States*, the official paper for the government, what many believed was the government's point of view regarding the Whiskey Rebellion. Thomas Jefferson and James Madison used other newspapers, such as the *Pennsylvanian Gazette* and *General Advertiser*, both from Philadelphia. While Jefferson and Madison agreed that Hamilton's policies, supported by the Federalists, were aristocratic by their very nature, they disagreed on the use of force against the people in western Pennsylvania. The raising of troops was unpopular, but when the Federalists labeled the Whiskey Boys as "Shaysites," and not vigilante farmers to drum up support for troops, patriot fever took hold. In a December 28, 1794 letter to Madison, Jefferson not only wrote against this, but also the way in which the Federalists attempted to quiet the media and the Democratic societies.

The Democratic societies formed in support of the people's causes. Their main purposes were promoting citizen awareness, public education, and public political discussions.[17] Along the western frontier, they petitioned the government to open the Mississippi River, and supported the people in their rights no matter how they chose to exercise them. In the East, they criticized the excise tax, but denounced the Whiskey Boys for their armed resistance. The Federalists tried at every opportunity to quiet the societies, and to limit or do away with their influence on the public, which did not always work. The Democratic societies involved in the western counties of Pennsylvania were the Mingo Creek and the Democratic Society of the County of Washington in Pennsylvania. The stronger of the two was the Mingo Creek Society. Established February 28, 1794, they spoke in exaggerated terms of liberty. Members elected each other to public office or influenced elections, and sometimes, were able to keep things out of the courts. The other society, located in Washington County, and formed in approximately March 1794, included prominent citizens as officers, such as James Marshal and David Bradford. Members of the Mingo Creek Society and the Washington Society were part of the vigilantes who burned John Neville's house in July 1794.

George Washington supported Hamilton regarding quelling the rebellion. He said the "insurrection" was the "first ripe fruit of the Democratic Societies," and wrote to John Jay that the Whiskey Boys "precipitated a crisis for which they were not prepared."[18] Jefferson showed his displeasure regarding the side Washington took when, in his December letter to Madison, he wrote, "It is wonderful indeed that the President should have permitted himself to be the organ of such an attack on the freedom of discussion." Washington thought that the Whiskey Boys would destroy the union created by the Revolutionary War if allowed to continue with their violent uprising. His position regarding the use of the military to handle a civil event was the first real stretch of the executive branch's right to order and lead troops.

Elected representatives from western Pennsylvania and other counties met at Parkinson's Ferry on August 14, 1794. Albert Gallatin, a representative in the Pennsylvania Assembly, opposed David Bradford's proposal to raise arms against the government leaders in eastern Pennsylvania.[19] The peace process began with Mr. Gallatin's speech, and they drew up a resolution[20] that

Figure 1 *Washington Reviewing the Western Army, at Fort Cumberland, Maryland.* Oil on canvas attributed to Frederick Kemmelmeyer. The Metropolitan Museum of Art.

promised protection to the people and property involved with the tax collection.

However, leaders in the East believed the gathering was an insurrection, and in October 1794, Washington ordered troops sent to the area.

Conclusion

The people of western Pennsylvania did not think troops would come, or if they did, they could intimidate them the way they did the tax collectors and all those that opposed them. For this reason, Generals Henry Lee and Hamilton met no resistance when they arrived with their fourteen thousand troops. In the end, the government required participants of the Whiskey Rebellion to sign an "Oath of Submission to the Laws of the United States" if they wished amnesty for their part in what transpired.[21] David Bradford and some of the other rebellion leaders fled to Ohio. The troops arrested thirty-two men, and marched them to Philadelphia for trial. The court only convicted two, John Mitchell, charged with mail robbery, and Philip Wigle, a known participant of a Fayette County riot, because they viewed the farmers as poor country bumpkins. George Washington eventually pardoned all of the Whiskey Rebellion participants except David Bradford.

Feelings ran deep regarding the Whiskey Rebellion. Generations fought over the truth of what happened and why. Brackenridge wrote about his activities during the rebellion for the side of the people, and about Neville's connection with the side of the government. Neville's grandson, Neville B. Craig, dismissed Brackenridge's story when he wrote his history of Pittsburgh. In response, Brackenridge's son wrote his own history to counter Craig's version.

The Whiskey Rebellion was two forms of rebellion that the Federalists would not tolerate. They considered meetings, such as the ones in Pittsburgh, as extra legal, even though they were peaceful, and produced only resolutions and written protests against the government. While the Federalists leaders overlooked the community censure and rebuke of taxpayers and collectors, the violence to people and property was too much to ignore. Hamilton wrote a narrative regarding the government's use of force, and stated that it was justified and moderated, and that it helped to end the rebellion. His spin on the authority of the president to use the military on internal issues helped establish the right to do so.

Notes

1. William Hogeland, *The Whiskey Rebels: George Washington, Alexander Hamilton, and the Frontier Rebels Who Challenged America's Newfound Sovereignty* (New York: A Lisa Drew Book/Scribner, 2006), 54.

2. Jerry A. Clouse, *The Whisky Rebellion: Southwestern Pennsylvania's Frontier People Test the American Constitution* (Harrisburg: Commonwealth of Pennsylvania Bureau for Historic Preservation Pennsylvania Historical and Museum Commission, 1994), 7.

3. Ronald P. Formisano, *For the People: American Populist Movements from the Revolution to the 1850's* (Chapel Hill: University of North Carolina Press, 2008), 49.

4. Leland D. Baldwin, *Whiskey Rebels: The Story of a Frontier Uprising* (Pittsburgh: University of Pittsburgh Press, 1939), 72.

5. Ibid., 57.

6. Ibid., 25.

7. Clouse, *Southwestern Pennsylvania's Frontier People*, 11.

8. Leland D. Baldwin, *Whiskey Rebels*, 68-69.

9. Ronald P. Formisano, *For the People*, 41-48.

10. Michael P. Hanagan, Leslie P. Moch, and Wayne P. Brake, *Challenging Authority: The Historical Study of Contentious Politics* (Minneapolis: The University of Minnesota Press, 1998), "Introduction," xxi.

11. Hanagan, Moch, and Brake, *Challenging Authority*, 38.

12. Clouse, *Southwestern Pennsylvania's Frontier People*, 17-18.

13. Ibid., 8.

14. Leland D. Baldwin, *Whiskey Rebels*, 62.

15. Ibid., 71.

16. Ibid., 12.

17. Ronald P. Formisano, *For the People*, 53.

18. Ibid., 51.

19. Clouse, *Southwestern Pennsylvania's Frontier People*, 31-33.

20. Parkinson's Ferry Meeting, Resolutions, *Document No. 1.*

21. Hanagan, Moch, and Brake, *Challenging Authority*, 40.

BIBLIOGRAPHY

Primary Sources

Parkinson's Ferry Meeting, Resolutions as proposed by Mr. Marshal and as adopted,
     August 14, 1794, "Document No. I." *Memoirs of the Historical Society of
     Pennsylvania, Vol. VI.* Philadelphia: J. B. Lippincott & Co., 1858.

Wilkins, John. Letter to William Irvine, August 19, 1794, "The Gathering of the
     Insurgents on Braddock's Field." *Memoirs of the Historical Society of
     Pennsylvania, Vol. VI.* Philadelphia: J. B. Lippincott & Co., 1858.

Secondary Sources

Baldwin, Leland D. *Whiskey Rebels: The Story of a Frontier Uprising.* Pittsburgh:
     University of Pittsburgh Press, 1939.

Clouse, Jerry A. *The Whisky Rebellion: Southwestern Pennsylvania's Frontier
     People Test the American Constitution.* Harrisburg: Commonwealth of
     Pennsylvania Bureau for Historic Preservation Pennsylvania Historical and
     Museum Commission, 1994.

Formisano, Ronald P. *For the People: American Populist Movements from the
     Revolution to the 1850's.* Chapel Hill: University of North Carolina Press,
     2008.

Hanagan, Michael P., Leslie P. Moch, and Wayne P. Brake. *Challenging Authority:
     The Historical Study of Contentious Politics.* Minneapolis: University of
     Minnesota Press, 1998.

Hogeland, William. *The Whiskey Rebels: George Washington, Alexander Hamilton,
     and the Frontier Rebels Who Challenged America's Newfound Sovereignty.*
     New York: A Lisa Drew Book/Scribner, 2006.

Knight, David C. *The Whiskey Rebellion, 1794: Revolt in Pennsylvania Threatens
     American Unity.* New York: Franklin Watts, Inc., 1968.

Smith, James Morton, ed. *The Republic of Letters: The Correspondence Between
     Thomas Jefferson and James Madison 1776-1826.* Volume Two, 1790-
     1804. New York: W. W. Norton & Company, Inc., 1995.

The Monroe Doctrine: Repealing European Control in the Americas

Ken Oziah

How did the Monroe Doctrine affect the United States' relations with the European powers? What was its impact on the new nation's trade and commerce? The Monroe Doctrine represented a position adopted by President James Monroe during his seventh annual address to Congress on 2 December 1823, which stated that the United States would oppose overtures by European powers against former and now independent colonies of Spain and Portugal in the Western Hemisphere. British Foreign Minister George Canning had proposed that Britain and the United States act together to prevent the resurgence of Bourbon power in the region; however, Monroe, abiding by the counsel of his Secretary of State, John Quincy Adams, chose to act unilaterally. As the policy served Great Britain's interests and the US was militarily weak relative to European powers, the Royal Navy served as the primary enforcer of the policy.

To understand how the Monroe Doctrine, as the policy came to be called, originated, one must first look at the continent of Europe after the fall of Louis Napoleon. In reaction to the wars with revolutionary France, on 26 September 1815, Austria, Prussia, and Russia entered into a treaty known as the Holy Alliance. Through the treaty, they sought to reestablish the control of absolute monarchies on the continent. Other European powers quickly signed the accord, including the re-established monarchy of France. France soon took measures to restore the former Spanish King, Ferdinand, to power in Spain as Ferdinand VII in 1823. As the Bourbon monarchies reestablished control, matters concerning the former Spanish colonies in the Western Hemisphere came under considerable discussion. The United States' Minister to Great Britain, Richard Rush, participated in lengthy correspondence and visits with British Foreign Secretary George Canning to discuss the potential impact of the Holy Alliance upon the Americas.

Amongst the European powers, only Great Britain and Rome did not sign the Holy Alliance accord—all the others eventually signed the compact. One provision of the treaty, which greatly concerned the Anglo-American powers, was a section that bound all parties to support and defend dynastic houses, and to assist one another to repel revolutions and rebellion.[1] Just how this pact would play out in recovering lost colonies in the Americas, was not clear; however, the battle of Trocadero, on 31 August 1823, sealed the fate of the constitutionalists in Spain, and set the stage for monarchy's return to Spain.

The great powers of Europe, having lent support to France for the invasion of Spain and the restoration of absolute monarchism by Ferdinand VII, did not stop there. The issue of the former Spanish colonies was foremost in the minds of many government ministers. Diplomatic discussions between Canning and Rush concerned matters of the Spanish Americas from time to time, but not as often as Rush desired. In fact, after the fall of Cadiz in Spain, there was not any conversation between Canning and Rush regarding the topic.[2] Rush felt that Britain concerned itself with commerce more than justice for the people of the continent of Europe, as well as the residents of South America.[3]

It was clear that Britain's interests in South America were purely economic. The Napoleonic War in Europe, as well as the continental system Napoleon installed, greatly decreased the amount of goods exported from Great Britain. England was in the midst of its industrial revolution, which meant it created greater means of production as well as greater stocks of goods. Exports were steadily decreasing to the continent, however, while exports increased to the former Spanish colonies.[4] The United States was interested in gaining trade with the new nations in South America, as well.

President Monroe extended diplomatic recognition of the new nations in South America, sending diplomats and extending the courtesy to the new national heads of state to send diplomats to Washington, D.C.[5] While discussions between Rush and Canning continued through the fall, they fell off markedly after late September 1823. President Monroe sought the advice of former Presidents Thomas Jefferson and James Madison with regard to a possible cooperative statement with Great Britain.[6] Jefferson and Madison appeared in favor of some sort of joint statement with Britain regarding European interference in South America.

Secretary of State John Quincy Adams, was in favor of a unilateral statement, having reservations concerning British intentions. He did not want to appear, "as a cock boat in the wake of a British man-of-war."[7] It appears even as far back as 1823, the United States considered annexing Texas, as well as Cuba. Still, the matter of possible invasion by members of the Holy Alliance was a real threat. The Holy Alliance decided that representative government was incompatible with the principles of monarchical sovereignty and divine right.[8] If they were successful in their efforts with Spain, what was to stop them from attempting to revert former colonies to Spanish rule?

On 9 October 1823, France and Britain signed the Polignac Memorandum, in which France agreed not to seek colonial possession of former Spanish colonies in South America. This was, of course, the reason for Canning's lack of continued interest in seeking a joint statement against European aggression in South America.

Figure 1 *James Monroe 1758-1860.* Oil on canvas by Rembrandt Peale, 1817-1825. James Monroe Museum and Memorial Library, Fredericksburg, Virginia.

This situation still concerned the United States' interests in Latin America. A French fleet might still sail towards the Americas, though the agreement France had with Britain against intervention was still new. This was the setting in October 1823, when President Monroe began considering the situation and possible statement on the matter.

Thomas Edington, in his book *The Monroe Doctrine,* states British Foreign Minister Canning as the real behind-the-scenes creator of the Monroe Doctrine.[9] It was Canning's belief that a bold statement against intervention by European powers into South America was a necessity. Of course, the British backed this belief based on purely economic factors. The United States, through its ministers to Britain as well as Secretary of State Adams, believed action was necessary to curtail possible involvement of the Holy Alliance into reclaiming former Spanish territory.

James Fawcett, in *The Origin and Text of the Monroe Doctrine,* points out that the Holy Alliance announced after the subjugation of the Spanish revolt, that

Spain intended to conquer Spanish American states. Therefore, on 2 December 1823, in a joint session of Congress, President James Monroe declared any attempt by European powers to extend their system of government to any portion of the Western Hemisphere as, "dangerous to our peace and safety."[11] This became one of the most important pieces of international diplomacy for the next 170 years.

The United States Navy was still relatively young compared to the British Navy, which was at the height of its power. It was clear that the British Navy was partially responsible for enforcing the tenets of the Monroe Doctrine.[12] In a letter to former President Thomas Jefferson, former President James Madison stated, "with the British power and navy combined with ours, we have nothing to fear from the rest of the world."[13]

In regards to Latin America, Foreign Secretary Canning engaged in negotiations with Prince de Polignac of France. These placed the British Navy in the center of the potential battle map. Fearing the power of the British Navy, France did not seek to pursue any attempts to colonize or control Latin America.[14] Every nation was aware Britain maintained the largest navy in the world and the members of the Holy Alliance did not want to tangle with Britain on international waters.[15]

British Honduras, later known as Belize, became an area of concern after the implementation of the Monroe Doctrine. Britain initially set up Belize as a logging settlement. Spain argued against the settlement, and later destroyed it. After quite some time, a few of the initial settlers who survived the destruction of the settlement and imprisonment in Cuba returned to rebuild the settlement. Under the consideration of the Monroe Doctrine, this area existed as a prior settlement of the British.[16]

Another incident in the area of Belize occurred at the Bay Islands. In this case, years after the British formally documented their claims to Belize, Britain decided to lay claim to the Bay Islands as a part of Belize. Great Britain and the United States dispatched war ships to the area, and it became an intense subject of negotiations between Britain and the United States, with the United States Minister to England, James Buchanan, taking a leading role. During negotiations, the United States invoked the Monroe Doctrine and Great Britain eventually turned over the Bay Islands to Honduras, who claimed right of ownership.[17]

The next major test of the Monroe Doctrine occurred during the American Civil War. Embroiled in battle, the United States was in no position to enforce the

Monroe Doctrine upon the French. France, under Napoleon III, took control of Mexico, on the premise of suspension of interest payments to Mexico's main creditors—Spain, France, and Britain. Napoleon III installed a new Bourbon familial Emperor, Don Maximilian, who was an Austrian Habsburg. The problem with the situation in Mexico was the $12 million debt in bonds held by France. France goaded Britain and Spain into assisting them with taking control of Vera Cruz, in an attempt to protect bondholders in their respective countries. Britain and Spain handled their affairs in Mexico, but the French ambition soon became known when France installed Maximilian on an imperial throne of Mexico.[18]

After the conclusion of the American Civil War, United States Secretary of State, William Seward, began intense correspondence with the Minister Bigelow of France. The situation took care of itself with the capture and execution of Maximilian during a revolution in 1867.[19] This effectively ended French involvement in Mexican affairs, as the French troops withdrew before the fall of Maximilian.

Throughout the history of Latin America, since throwing off the mantle of absolute monarchs, anarchy mixed with democracy and despotism. The history of Mexico alone is rife with revolutions and new governments. Attempting to model their government after the United States and its Constitution, failure after failure fell upon their heads. New Granada, now known as Colombia, also has a rich history of strife and revolution. She had three other sections break away and become nations unto themselves. Peru, Venezuela, and Panama were all once part of Colombia.

The institution of the Monroe Doctrine through the nineteenth century ensured Latin America's ability to determine its own destiny. However, lack of cooperation and consensus continued to breed one revolution after another. Without the Monroe Doctrine, Latin America would surely have come under the control of European powers, such as Spain and France. One has to wonder if Latin America would have been better off with reverting to colonial status, if even for a number of decades.

The Monroe Doctrine also prohibited foreign powers that held control of territories in the Americas from transferring those territories to other foreign powers.[20] An area of interest is the colonization of New Zealand and Fiji. In his book, Edington made little mention of this situation, and the United States did not object to the control of either island by Great Britain.[21]

The Monroe Doctrine was an attempt to curtail the involvement of European powers in North, Central, and South America. The view of neutrality long held by the government of the United States served to keep the fledgling nation out of the entangling affairs of the continent of Europe and secure trade for her commerce as a neutral state. This doctrine served United States foreign policy from 2 December 1823, into the twentieth century.

Notes

1. Thomas B. Edington, *The Monroe Doctrine* (Cambridge, Mass: University Press, 1904), 2.

2. Ibid., 23.

3. Ibid., 23.

4. Leonard A. Lawson, *The relation of British policy to the declaration of the Monroe doctrine* (New York: Columbia University, 1922), 78-80.

5. Mark T. Gilderhus, "The Monroe Doctrine: Meanings and Implications," *Presidential Studies Quarterly* 36, no. 1 (March 2006): 7.

6. Ibid., 7.

7. Ibid., 7.

8. James W. Fawcett, "*The Origin and Text of the Famous Monroe Doctrine*," *Congressional Digest* 18, no. 3 (March 1939): 74.

9. Edington, 51.

10. Fawcett, 75.

11. James Monroe, "Seventh Annual Message, "Messages *and Papers of the Presidents, James Monroe, Vol. 1*, 776.

12. Gilderhus, 8.

13. Lawson, 127.

14. Ibid., 137.

15. Ibid., 143.

16. Edington, 60-64. The Monroe Doctrine never contested the area known as British Honduras.

17. Ibid., 65-67. The decision to return the Bay Islands to Honduras narrowly averted war between Britain and the United States on the premise of the Monroe Doctrine.

18. Ibid., 121.

19. Ibid., 74. The fact that the United States was embroiled in a bitter civil war allowed France to enter Mexico without any correspondence or warning by the United States with regard to the Monroe Doctrine.

20. Ibid., 97.

21. Ibid., 103.

BIBLIOGRAPHY

Edington, Thomas B. *The Monroe Doctrine*. Cambridge, Mass: The University
        Press, 1904.

Gilderhus, Mark T. "The Monroe Doctrine: Meanings and Implications."
        Presidential Studies Quarterly 36, no. 1 (March 2006): 5-16.

Lawson, Leonard A. *The relation of British policy to the declaration of the
        Monroe doctrine*. New York: Columbia University, 1922.

Monroe, James. "Monroe Doctrine." *Monroe Doctrine* (January 17, 2009):1.

Waldo Fawcett, James. "The Origin and Text of the Famous Monroe Doctrine."
        Congressional Digest 18, no. 3 (March 1939): 74-77.

The French Intervention in Mexico

Lawrence Graves

The role of the United States on the global stage has been a subject of study and debate for many years. America's dominant role in today's world is now generally agreed upon, but what about its entrance into this global arena? When did this debut actually occur? Since there has been no official certificatory body to award a global power designation, the occasion that saw America's emergence as a world power is up for debate. Although obscured by high-profile world wars, regional wars, and perhaps other incidents, it was America's response to a direct threat of its Monroe Doctrine, that in the form of the French intervention in Mexico, which marks America's first significant entry into the global power community. Its effect on the Second French Empire would ripple throughout the world wherever France established her interests and ultimately alter the forthcoming regime change in France. America's action also had a hand in reversing a new wave of colonization that was beginning in Mexico; this too had an effect on global relations that could have grown between Mexico and other nations around the world.

Many have considered America's entrance into the First World War as her first global power emergence. Richard Worth, an author of high school level textbooks, expressed this generally accepted view, which sums up the common belief that "through its participation in World War I, the United States became an important international world power."[1] Such a statement made to youthful readers, who will perhaps never approach the subject again, underscores the widespread acceptance of this view. Such a view does have its merits. American troops, and their impressive support network, started to arrive in France just in time to prop up their wavering allies, and then took the battle to Imperial Germany's armies. After the war and President Wilson's retreat from the Paris Peace Conference, the United States opted for a more isolationist foreign policy.[2] The Senate's refusal to ratify the Versailles Treaty, and thereby join the League of Nations, only left American finance as its significant force in the global world. While the view of the First World War's importance to the history of global power is unquestioned, it was decades removed from America's maiden entry into the ranks of global powers.

The end of the nineteenth century saw another episode that historians can cite as America's entry into a more global status. The 1898 conflict most commonly referred to as the "Spanish-American War" was such an episode. The United States projected its military power to the nearby island of Cuba and the far-off archipelago of the Philippines. Its chief result: a colonial acquisition of the Philippines, after putting down a spirited native insurgency, and additional islands in the Pacific and the Caribbean, had a far longer lasting legacy for the United States than the toothless treaties ending the First World War or establishing the League of Nations that America would never join.

Some believed the 1898 war with Spain was the catalyst that ushered America into the ranks of global power states. In the decade after that war's end, Harvard University professor of history, Archibald Coolidge, summarized the result of the war: "It was evident that they [the United States] had assumed a new position among nations; that henceforth they would have to be counted with as one of the chief forces in international affairs."[3] The 1898 war, and the Philippines' rebellion against an American change in ownership, tied America to a global wheel that would turn to further issues. The importance of that epoch continues to be recognized by historians today. David Haglund also agrees with the view that in the time of Teddy Roosevelt's ascendancy, America entered the world stage as a "world power, but had not yet emerged as a 'superpower.'"[4] Perhaps the degree of power America wielded during that epoch might be a matter of debate, but the fact that America had arrived onto the world stage at that time is less debatable. An assessment within the last decade by Neil Smith has a similar evaluation of the 1898 war and subsequent successful conquests undertaken by the United States: "the Spanish American War . . . also marks the cusp of a radically different globalism. The symbolic dawn of the American Century"[5] was underway with the aggressive action of the United States; an action that was noticeably quick through the agency of an attack against Spain, a global power in decline.[6]

Among many historians, it seems agreed that the 1898 war and its aftermath marks the beginning of an era, an "American Century" as some would call it. Was there yet another time, previous to even the Spanish War, that saw America wielding power with a global force? Had that bold Yankee assertion already inserted itself unto the world stage some time before?

The declaration of the Monroe Doctrine in 1823 changed the way that

America would deal with its neighbors and the great powers across the Atlantic. Alfred Bushnell Hart points to the idea of doctrine's global significance in regards to American policy. "The Monroe doctrine was founded on the idea of a territorial division of the world into two separate hemispheres."[7] The globe was thus divided into two views and two American foreign policies. The United States would no longer, in principle at least, limit herself to responding to direct attacks upon her soil or citizenry, as in 1812. The adolescent nation was beginning to demand more attention from its more mature forebears.

After America proclaimed the Monroe Doctrine, whatever a European nation did to alter the governance of any American nation, be it Mexico or Honduras, and later even South America, would be a concern of the United States.[8] Isolationist tendencies, always strong in America, still would not overrule this issue. The Atlantic Ocean provided a buffer against the Old World, but not so for concerns emanating from the Americas. If the European powers that had reached around the globe wished to change the existing order in the New World, the United States would have to emerge from its continental fortress and engage such a world power, thereby globalizing American potential after 1823.

The evolution of the doctrine's idea into an actual force affecting the global balance of power would come into being in 1865. The American Civil War, that bloody four-year-long cataclysm, would provide the impetus for a European monarch, Louis-Napoleon Bonaparte of France, known to history as Napoleon III, nephew of the great Napoleon Bonaparte, to openly flaunt the Monroe Doctrine. At that time, the risk of war with the United States was not likely, as these same states were greatly pre-occupied in a war with each other. If the United States ceased to exist, there would be an opportunity to fill in the vacuum of power and influence it had left, but which nation would be bold enough to grasp it?

Napoleon III's desire to compete with the United Kingdom for economic and imperial ascendancy enticed him into an adventure in the New World.[9] Those in the French press, such as Alphonse de Lamartine, argued the emperor's goal was "to obtain, not for France alone, but for Europe at large, a foothold upon the American continent."[10] The concerns of several countries complicated the entire Mexican affair, though France would shoulder the greatest burden, and subsequent consequences. The catalyst for setting this "new Napoleonic Vision"[11] into motion was the status of the United States. After Confederate forces fired on Fort Sumter, the adolescent American power had suddenly turned upon itself. The consequences of such changes were tremendous—along with the rewards for those bold enough, or desperate enough, to step into the power vacuum. If the United States disintegrated, a major world power such as France would have a literally golden opportunity to tap into the immense wealth of the Americas, a wealth that had only recently been wrenched free from European imperial control.

A captain of the French officer corps, the comte Émile de Kératry, who would participate in the Mexican adventure, wrote about the reasons the French believed they went to Mexico in the first place—and the United States was at the heart of this reasoning. "It was the apparent dissolution of the United States which has been at the origin of the Mexican venture, just as their resurrection was sufficient to annihilate this ephemeral throne."[12] As the Civil War grew fiercer and more prolonged, the seemingly imminent collapse of the United States drew a global power player into the periphery of the borderlands and conflict, waiting for the right time to strike.

During this crucial time in the mid-nineteenth century, a sudden disruption of American cotton exports coincided with the explosion of textile manufacturing, and in itself signaled heightened American influence on the global stage. England knew this time as the "Cotton Famine," and the Union blockade of Southern cotton exports during the Civil War years severely crippled Britain's great textile industry.[13] Britain and others scrambled to increase cotton production in areas such as India and Egypt. The United States caused this global disturbance, which was an unintended consequence of a military policy designed to win a domestic war. However, Louis Napoleon's flaunting of the Monroe Doctrine during and after the same war warranted direct action by the United States. The consequences of this action would set the Second French Empire on a downward slide that would culminate in its overthrow in 1871, resulting in Napoleon III's capture by the Prussians and the establishment of the Third French Republic. Not only was the Second French Empire damaged by America's threatened use of force but Americans forced Europeans and others who flocked to Mexico to leave, and in doing so, severed the establishment of potential global connections.

By threatening France, a global power, the United States altered the global balance of power. The Second French Empire, having been thrown off guard in Mexico, was not fully able to meet the threat from Prussia's Bismarck that soon crippled French interest on the continent vis-à-vis Prussia's attacks on Denmark and then Austria herself.[14] A still unprepared France fell to Prussia just a few years following the French pullout from Mexico and America had a hand in that result. The *honneur* of the French Army had suffered; a flagging morale would follow. Hazen comments on the Mexican Affair that: "It had damaged him [Louis Napoleon] morally before Europe [and elsewhere] by the desertion of his protégés to an appalling fate before the threats of the United States."[15] The damage to Napoleon III's prestige revealed cracks in the armor of the French behemoth that the likes of Bismarck would exploit. The world had seen how the threats from the United States had forced the mighty Second French Empire to back down.

Napoleon III thought he could rectify his sagging fortunes by saber-rattling against the Prussians, but Bismarck was ready for any and all of his actions. The Prussian chancellor engineered events that would culminate in the Franco-Prussian War.[16] That would be the last war that Napoleon III would fight, and its result would not be the same as his namesake had achieved at Jena decades before. Prussia defeated France, and Napoleon became a prisoner who would then die in exile a few years later. The Second French Empire simply would not survive.[17] France was not excluded from further global power however, for it reinvented its imperial vision under its new government, the Third Republic. From that time forward there would be no French monarch, Bonaparte or otherwise, to command the homeland or its far-flung colonies. In place of royalist adventurers, there came efficient republican bureaucrats who had more success than that experienced by any of Louis-Napoleon's administrators. How did events in Mexico become so important for the United States, France, and the world at large? During the early years of the American Civil War, the great European powers, France, Great Britain, and Spain, landed troops in Mexico, as had happened before, thanks to the anarchy that had gripped this unhappy nation for the previous forty years.[18] Although they claimed to have taken this action of forcing Mexico to resume the debt payments to the European nations it had defaulted on, it in fact turned out to be a scheme of the French emperor to establish a new monarchy in Mexico. This was to be a power base that would expand European influence in the Americas in direct opposition to the Monroe Doctrine. Kératry sums up well what was in Napoleon III's mind at the beginning of the Mexican adventure:

> Since the United States already appeared non-existent, since the coast was clear in the New World, why not attempt something big, which although not useless to the French interest, would certainly *enhance the prestige so needed by its government* [emphasis added]. They had, against Mexico; endless grievances...why not go with weapons in hand to demand

reparation of those grievances, like it had been done several times already? But this time, we could not appear on these distant coasts and leave with a treaty, nor could we just occupy a port and receive the necessary indemnities. This time our arrival should signal the start of a revolution. . . This revolution, which [conservative Mexican] immigrants full of confidence thought would be certain and easy, was supposed to overthrow the republic and result in the foundation of a throne with our support.[19]

When the British and Spanish realized Napoleon III had plans beyond a demand for reparations, they recalled their troops. The French stayed on, and sent more troops.

While the French and their allies were busy conquering Mexico, in 1864, Mexican exiles in France and Napoleon III invited Maximilian von Hapsburg, the brother of the Emperor of Austria, to come and be emperor of Mexico, which his troops already occupied.[20] The Austrian prince was to secure a new power base, a Latin power base that a Hapsburg could

Figure 1. The Mexican Delegation Offering the Mexican Imperial Crown to Maximilian of Hapsburg. Painting by Cesare dell'Acqua, 1863.

still accomplish. Anglo-America would have a Franco-Latin counterbalance— and that from a Germanic monarch in the Western Hemisphere. But the growth in the global relations that could have been fostered fell away as their French protectors turned away in the face of American hostility.

When a delegation of exiled Mexican conservatives came to Austria to offer the Hapsburg prince a crown as their emperor, they augmented the offer with a certain promise. The French emperor promised additional troops, on top of the few Austrian and Belgian troops already contracted to the cause. Also adding impetus was a flimsy plebiscite that only polled those conservative Mexicans most likely to agree; it stated Maximilian was to rule the will of the Mexican people. This finally convinced the young prince and his consort, Charlotte, to board a ship for the

Mexican port city of Veracruz. From there, they began the march that would end in the president's palace in Mexico City.[21]

By 1865, the Europeans and their allies had overrun almost all of Mexico. They forced Benito Juárez, the legally-elected president of Mexico, to flee to Mexico's northern border to conduct a guerilla war. It seemed as if Napoleon III's scheme would come to fruition until the American Civil War ended with a victory for the Union forces. From then on in Mexico, the tables started to turn. The Mexican Republican forces started receiving American aid, including many surplus Civil War weapons, veteran fighters, and non-material aid that propped up the republican cause.[22]

America's covert and overt actions countered European efforts in Mexico, and the fact that Napoleon attempted to erect a European-led monarchy on the ruins of the Mexican republic, called for a bold American stroke to defend the Monroe Doctrine. What made this action so daring was that American leaders, so soon after the bloodiest conflict in the country's history, had the fortitude to risk a war with a major world power to enforce a doctrine that some argued to be insignificant on the domestic scene.

As the imperialists realized that few in their country were going to embrace the usurpation of the elected Mexican government by foreigners and their armies, the need arose for more European troops to arrive and firmly establish the Second Mexican Empire by force. In total, France sent more than 38,000 French troops, representing twenty percent of Napoleon III's armed forces, to Mexico. This, however, was not a strictly French affair. The Khedive of Egypt sent some 450 Sudanese soldiers. Austria sent approximately 7,000 troops, while Belgium added about 2,000 volunteers known as *"le régiment Impératrice Charlotte."*[23] Maximilian's consort was Belgian, and he formed the Belgian volunteer regiment in her name. Since these troops received pay for their service, they more properly might have been called mercenaries. Whatever their label, they were part of an international force with a common enemy: the Mexican Republican forces, regular and guerilla, under Juárez.

Thus the United States threatened to go to war against a global coalition, but its greatest pressure selectively targeted the French. America directed her full diplomatic and military weight against the French forces; since without French soldiers, the remaining soldiers of the other nationalities would evacuate without reinforcements. When Napoleon decided at last to call his troops home in stages, he did try to arrange for additional Austrian troops to fill their void. America immediately threatened Austria with war. Austria backed down.[24] Vienna had a growing concern that Berlin would target them next, even though they had been allied against Denmark not long before. Berlin's aggression would soon yield devastating results to Austria's once-great continental power.

As expected, all the other troops, along with many colonists Maximilian had invited, fled Mexico when the French regiments, there protecting them, started to leave.[25] Mexicans sympathetic to Juárez, increasingly the majority of the country, would make little distinctions in nationalities when carrying out reprisals against those they saw in their country to aid a foreign power poised against them.

By the start of 1867, those who had come to Mexico to prop up or benefit from the imperial throne began to desert that same throne— the emperor of the French would be no exception. The nineteenth century English historian, W. H. Adams, notes that the desertion of Maximilian by Louis Napoleon in the face of American pressure "must ever remain a dark stain on the history of the second French empire."[26] Because of this, Maximilian would pay with his life, while Napoleon would eventually pay with his throne. These events started when America decided to get involved with the currents affairs of Mexico.

The French emperor's desire to regain lost prestige would tempt him into war with Prussia in hopes that his subjects would rally around him in the time of war. The emperor was in need of a new, revamped image—what better way than to lead his nation into action against upstart Prussia in order to gain the "revenge for Sadowa" his subjects were clamoring for? Since "both the military and political prestige of Napoleon III were dimmed by the melancholy issue of the Mexican expedition"[27] there needed to be a war to return the glory to the throne that was sliding into jeopardy. There must have been a question in the minds of his subordinates: if Louis-Napoleon would leave a Hapsburg, the brother of the Emperor of Austria, in the lurch, how faithful would he be to anyone else he had need of that was perhaps less nobly born?

The enforcement of the Monroe Doctrine upon a global power, the Second Empire of France, compromised the power and legacy of the first Napoleon's greatness to a point of inaugurating the decline of France's domination of the European continent in the face of Prussia. Prussia, the unifier of Germany, would, in a few years, be celebrating the beginning of the Second German Reich in the halls of Versailles itself. Napoleon III's scheme at re-legitimization had backfired with the most disastrous of results.

The response to the French intervention was an important moment in the foreign policy history of the United States. American government leaders stood on principle when the nation could hardly afford to do so. It was a bold, decisive, and ultimately successful act remarkable when compared to the more common escalation's resultant bloodshed. Historians should study this incident more often and in more detail to instruct those today who may find themselves in a similar situation—having to choose between costly principle and easy expediency. It also deserves further investigation to understand more deeply how America's newly-aggressive posture affected the decisions of other nations, either militarily or economically.

America might have had only regional intentions when it started its saber -rattling, but its action against France had global repercussions. There was more than a military intervention taking place in Mexico at that time, a new wave of colonists, including Confederate soldiers and political leaders, had been arriving and settling in Mexico since before the end of the Civil War. As part of his perceived duties to promote the settlement of lands that earlier strife had depopulated, "Maximilian had made extensive land grants to German, French, and Austrian immigrants."[28] He had to divert imperial troops to protect these settlers. Those Mexicans not in Maximilian's camp viewed these settlers the same as the foreign soldiers that had come to force an unwanted throne upon them. When Napoleon III bowed to American pressure and started to recall his troops, these new settlers found it wise to leave the country before they would have to pay for the land they had been granted with their lives.[29] The native Mexicans who would take their lands back from these new settlers would not establish international connections, they only wanted to take back that which had been torn from them.

The displaced settlers, fresh from Europe and elsewhere, would have naturally established such connections for economic and other reasons, but this was not to be. The actions of the United States limited Mexico's development in what could have been a more varied global presence as a new round of immigrants, wealthier than the average pioneer farmer, were driven out of Mexico. The re-possessors of their land, who by in large were indigenous Indians, of course had no global contacts.[30] This was an unintended consequence of enforcing the Monroe Doctrine. There would be no new wave of immigration to

Mexico, thanks to American threats of military action and surplus American firearms that were increasingly finding their way into the hands of Mexican Juarista fighters.

The wars of the United States have often been the mileposts used by historians to divide its history. Anyone familiar with the history of the United States will at once know the general time frame being examined by its relation to a past or future war; the "ante-bellum" term is very familiar example to describe the years preceding the Civil War, along with the "interwar years" of the twentieth century. The Mexican affair was different; Americans did not experience any additional bloodshed so close on the heels of the Civil War. There were no banner headlines proclaiming its events, no returning troops to receive a hero's welcome as they would have marched down Pennsylvania Avenue. This affair was a success without the body counts, which has not attracted a great amount of re-examination.

America's response to European troops on its southern border may appear strictly regional to some, yet an examination of the events that occurred during this time will show that there were global consequences the original protagonists involved never dreamed of. From altered relations to the Holy See, which was never able to reclaim lands in Mexico confiscated from the Church, to the rolling back of European immigration and settlers who had come with Maximilian's blessing, the consequences were significant. The absence of actual hostilities and memorable battles perhaps has ensured that America's response to the French intervention in Mexico is little appreciated by those who study American or global history. Regardless, this was not only a crucial time in America's history, it would have impacts of global importance as the Monroe Doctrine was revived and strengthened, while at the same time the prestige of an emperor who ruled over a global empire was so damaged that soon its effects would remove him from the world's stage. Two empires, Mexican and French, fell and were permanently replaced by two republics. America had a hand in this and more.

Notes

1. Richard Worth, *America in World War I* (New York: World Almanac Library, 2007), 6.

2. Ole Holsti, *Public Opinion and American Foreign Policy*, rev. ed. (Ann Arbor: University of Michigan Press, 2009), 16, http://site.ebrary.com/lib/apus/docDetail.action?docID=10315953&p00=%22american%20isolationism%22 (accessed July 2, 2011).

3. Archibald Cary Coolidge, *The United States as a World Power* (New York: MacMillan & Co., 1908), 132.

4. David G. Haglund, "Devant L'Empire: France and the Question of 'American Empire,' from Theodore Roosevelt to George W. Bush," *Diplomacy & Statecraft* 19, no.4 (December 2008): 749, *Academic Search Premier*, EBSCO*host* (accessed July 16, 2011).

5. Neil Smith, *American Empire : Roosevelt's Geographer and the Prelude to Globalization* (Berkeley: University of California Press, 2003), 60, http:// site.ebrary.com/lib/apus/docDetail.action? docID=10062315&p00= %22american%20empire%22 (accessed July 21, 2011).

6. Scott Miller, *The President and the Assassin: McKinley, Terror, and Empire at the Dawn of the American Century* (New York: Random House, 2011), 216.

7. Alfred Bushnell Hart, *The Monroe Doctrine: an Interpretation* (Boston: Little, Brown & Co., 1916), 70.

8. Ibid., 75.

9. Sarah York Stevenson, *Maximilian in Mexico: a Woman's Reminiscences of the French Intervention in Mexico* (New York: Century Company, 1899), 3.

10. Ibid., 2.

11. Ibid., 7.

12. Emile de Kératry, *L'Élévation et la chute de l'empereur Maximilien: Histoire de L'intervention française au Mexique, 1861-1867,* trans. by Christine Gokey (Leipzig: Dunker et Humblot, 1867), x.

13. Brian Schoen, *Fragile Fabric of Union: Cotton, Federal Politics, and the Global Origins of the Civil War* (Baltimore: Johns Hopkins University Press, 2009), 267.

14. Charles Downer Hazen, *Modern European History* (New York: Henry Holt & Co., 1917), 353.

15. Ibid., 354.

16. Ibid., 356.

17. Ibid., 358.

18. Stevenson, *Maximilian in Mexico,* 11.

19. Kératry, *L'Élévation et la chute de l'empereur Maximilien,* xi.

20. Stevenson, 4.

21. Stevenson, *Maximilian in Mexico,* 3-7.

22. William E. Hardy, "South of the Border: Ulysses S. Grant and the French Intervention," *Civil War History* 54, no. 1 (March 2008): 64-67, *Academic Search Premier*, EBSCO*host* (accessed July 6, 2011).

23. "Expédition du Mexique 1861-1867," *Histoire du Monde.net,* http://www.histoiredumonde.net/article. php3?id_article=1201 (accessed July 6, 2011).

24. Stephen J. Valone, "'Weakness Offers Temptation': William H. Seward and the Reassertion of the Monroe Doctrine," *Diplomatic History* 4, no. 19 (Fall 1995), http://web.ebscohost.com (accessed July 14, 2011).

25. Stevenson, *Maximilian In Mexico*, 256.

26. Adams, W. H. Davenport, *Franco-Prussian War: Its Causes, Incidents, and Consequences,* ed. H. M. Hozier (London: W. Mackenzie, 1872), http:// www.archive.org/stream/francoprussianwa00hozi#page/n7/mode/2up (accessed July 3, 2011).

27. Ibid., 161.

28. Andrew F. Rolle, *The Lost Cause: the Confederate Exodus to Mexico* (Norman, OK: University of Oklahoma Press, 1965), 24.

29. Stevenson, 254.

30. Rolle, *The Lost Cause,* 110.

BIBLIOGRAPHY

Adams, W. H. Davenport. *Franco-Prussian War: Its Causes, Incidents, and Consequences.* Edited by H. M. Hozier. London: W. Mackenzie, 1872. http:// www.archive.org/stream/francoprussianwa00hozi#page/n7/ mode/2up (accessed July 3, 2011).

Coolidge, Archibald Cary. *The United States as a World Power.* New York: MacMillan & Co., 1908.

"Expédition du Mexique 1861-1867" *Histoire du Monde.net.* http:// www.histoiredumonde.net/article.php3?id_article=1201 (accessed July 6, 2011).

Haglund, David G. "Devant L'Empire: France and the Question of 'American Empire,' from Theodore Roosevelt to George W. Bush." *Diplomacy & Statecraft* 19, no.4 (December 2008): 746-766. *Academic Search Premier*, EBSCO*host* (accessed July 16, 2011).

Hardy, William E. "South of the Border: Ulysses S. Grant and the French Intervention." *Civil War History* 54, no. 1 (March 2008): 63-86. *Academic Search Premier*, EBSCO*host* (accessed July 6, 2011).

Hart, Alfred Bushnell. *The Monroe Doctrine: an Interpretation.* Boston: Little, Brown & Co., 1916.

Hazen, Charles Downer. *Modern European History.* New York: Henry Holt & Co., 1917.

Holsti, Ole. *Public Opinion and American Foreign Policy.* Rev. ed. Ann Arbor: University of Michigan Press, 2009. http://site.ebrary.com/lib/apus/ docDetail. action?docID=10315953&p00=%22american%20 isolationism%22 (accessed July 2, 2011).

Kératry, Émile de. *L'Élévation et la chute de l'empereur Maximilien: Histoire de L'intervention française au Mexique, 1861-1867.* Translated by Christine Gokey. Leipzig: Dunker et Humblot, 1867.

Miller, Scott. *The President and the Assassin: McKinley, Terror, and Empire at the Dawn of the American Century.* New York: Random House, 2011.

Reddaway, W.F. *The Monroe Doctrine.* Cambridge: Cambridge University Press, 1898.

Rolle, Andrew F. *The Lost Cause: the Confederate Exodus to Mexico.* Norman, OK: University of Oklahoma Press, 1965.

Schoen, Brian. *Fragile Fabric of Union: Cotton, Federal Politics, and the Global Origins of the Civil War.* Baltimore: Johns Hopkins University Press, 2009.

Smith, Neil, *American Empire: Roosevelt's Geographer and the Prelude to Globalization.* Berkeley: University of California Press, 2003. http://site.ebrary.com/lib/apus/docDetail.action?docID=10062315&p00=%22american%20empire%22 (accessed July 21, 2011).

Stevenson, Sara Yorke. *Maximilian in Mexico: a Woman's Reminiscences of the French Intervention in Mexico.* New York: Century Company, 1899.

Valone, Stephen J. "'Weakness Offers Temptation': William H. Seward and the Reassertion of the Monroe Doctrine." *Diplomatic History* 4, no. 19 (Fall 1995). http://web.ebscohost.com (accessed July 14, 2011).

Worth, Richard. *America in World War I.* New York: World Almanac Library, 2007.

Baptism of Fire: In Defense of Colonel Fribley and the 8th USCT

Jennifer Thompson

When a regiment suffers great losses in its first battle, its baptism of fire, many blame the regiment and its commander. The 8th United States Colored Troop (USCT) suffered the heaviest regimental loss in the battle of Olustee in the Civil War, yet this regiment and its colonel showed great courage under fire. According to Carlton McCarthy, a private in the Richmond Howitzers, a soldier must be brave in battle: "His courage must never fail. He must be manly and independent."[1] Black troops fought for more than manliness and independence; they fought for freedom.

At the beginning of the Civil War, the War Department felt blacks had no part in a "white man's war." Lincoln feared recruiting blacks would drive the border states into the Confederacy. After the First Battle of Bull Run, Lincoln allowed blacks to join the army as laborers and in other non-combat roles. In his book, *The African-American Soldier: From Crispus Attucks to Colin Powell*, Lt. Col. Michael Lanning explained, "African Americans were ready and willing to serve in the military where needed. This time, the war was *about,* and *over,* them."[2] The War Department established the Bureau of Colored Troops in May 1863. Although the army organized a few black regiments prior to this date, most black regiments formed after this date. These soldiers faced discrimination in pay and promotion. White privates received $13 a month, with pay increasing with rank. All black soldiers received only $10 a month, regardless of rank. White officers commanded black troops, while black soldiers could only become non-commissioned officers. Black soldiers proved to be well disciplined and served honorably. "While denied the rank of officer, black soldiers nonetheless displayed their leadership abilities under fire. . . . The African-American soldiers willingly assumed the responsibility of proving themselves, freeing their brothers, and preserving the Union."[3] To create fear in Union black troops, the Confederate Congress approved the death penalty for captured white officers of black troops and allowed states to punish the black soldiers. "Within three months of this congressional report, President Lincoln . . . vowed to execute one Confederate officer for every Union commander of black troops whom the Rebels might put to death and to sentence to hard labor one captured southern soldier for every black

Union trooper sold into slavery. The threat did not have to be carried out."[4] The Army established Camp William Penn, under the command of Louis Wagner, in Pennsylvania as the first U.S. black soldier recruiting and training center. Recruiting for the 8th USCT began in September 1863.[5]

Charles Wesley Fribley was an experienced soldier, who became commander of the 8th USCT. Fribley grew up on a farm in Pennsylvania and attended Dickinson Seminary in Williamsport. He moved to the West in 1857 to seek his fortune as a ferry boatman, schoolteacher, Overland Mail conductor, and fighter between "bleeding Kansas" and border ruffians. Fribley returned to Pennsylvania and became a teacher. A few days after the attack on Fort Sumter, Fribley answered Lincoln's call for volunteers and joined a three-month regiment – the Woodward Guards (Company A of the 11th Pennsylvania infantry). In mid-October 1861, Fribley enlisted in Company

Figure 1 Charles and Kate Fribley, 1861. From the author's personal collection.

F of the 84th Pennsylvania Infantry. "Felt that I could not be satisfied at the old and harassing business of today and furthermore that it was my duty to be with those of my countrymen who were in arms in defence [sic] of our flag."[6] On December 10, 1861, Fribley married Katherine "Kate" Ault. Colonel Samuel M. Bowman commended Fribley for his assistance as staff officer during the Chancellorsville Campaign in 1863: "The following staff officers of this command –Capt. Charles W. Fribley, Eighty-fourth Pennsylvania Volunteers, acting assistant adjutant-general; . . . rendered me the most valuable assistance on more than one trying occasion, and in the discharge of their duties displayed the utmost coolness and bravery."[7]

In 1863, Fribley made two major decisions, changing his life forever. Realizing that death might happen soon, Fribley settled his account with God in April 1863: "Read . . . 'How to Turn a Christian'. Did me much good. I this day choose to be and resolve to be a Christian."[8] On July 8, 1863, Fribley applied to the War Department for command of a black troop. The War Department established examination boards to qualify black troop officers: "The army hoped to assure the Union leadership that if the USCT regiments performed poorly, it was not because of any fault of their officers. The test examined the officers in six areas: tactics, regulations, general military knowledge, math, history, and geography."[9] On July 27, Fribley sent an additional application to report for the examination. On August 20, he received permission to report for the examination in Washington. He spent the next week studying and left August 31 for Washington. Candidates usually waited an additional week before appearing before the board: "Candidates reported promptly each morning and learned whether or not they would be tested that day. If they were too far down the list, the officer merely dismissed them for the day, and the process repeated the next day, Monday through Friday."[10] Fribley appeared before Major General Casey on September 19 and passed the board as "Colonel of first class."[11] On September 26, he received orders to report to Lieutenant Colonel Wagner. Fribley took command of the 8th USCT October 3.

For the next few months, Fribley drilled his regiment. "During drill the men had to learn various military commands that they would need in combat. They also had to be able to understand and execute commands quickly. On the battlefield, not following an order immediately could mean injury or death."[12] Fribley held Marshal and Sergeant's school in the evenings of November. After recruiting ten companies, Fribley officially received his appointment as colonel on November 23 and spent that day mustering in and purchasing his new uniform. The next few days, he raised money for supplies for the regiment and found musicians for the band. The 8th USCT moved into wooden army barracks in December 1863. Fribley purchased musical instruments and two howitzers, organized companies, and continued drills throughout December. "The sham battle was quite good indeed considering the fact of there being no artillery."[13] January 7 brought frustration to Fribley and his wife when they went to Philadelphia by train for business and to run errands. Fribley felt disappointed by the amount of his pay. He and his wife got separated. Fribley spent a lot of time searching for her and finally found her in the train cars. Later that day, a conflict arose between Fribley and Wagner: "Had unpleasant words with Col. Wagner."[14] The band made their first appearance at dress parade on January 8, 1864. That same day, Lieutenant Colonel Louis Wagner charged Colonel Fribley with disobedience of orders "beating calls for Church, Drill and Tattoo at unestablished hours" and conduct "unbecoming an officer and a gentleman" for his response to the original charges: "tell Col. Wagner to attend to his own business and he [Col. F.] would attend to his."[15] The Acting Judge Advocate did not feel the charges important enough to warrant a trial before him.

On January 9, the regiment received marching orders. They left camp on January 16 for New York, where they boarded two transports, the *Prometheus* and the *City of Bath*. The *City of Bath* arrived at Hilton Head, South Carolina on January 22. The *Prometheus* encountered stormy weather, causing many officers including Fribley, to become seasick. The *Prometheus*, after a stop at Fort Monroe, arrived at Hilton Head on January 24. The 8th USCT was assigned to Howell's Brigade, Seymour's Division, Gillmore's Department. Fribley continued to drill his men with a dress parade on January 27, inspection on January 28, brigade drill on January 29, and battalion drill on January 30. Kate accompanied her husband to Hilton Head and stayed until the regiment left for Florida on February 6. Gillmore planned to secure Florida: to gain supplies of cotton, turpentine, and timber; to cut off enemy supplies; to obtain colored recruits; and to restore Florida to the Union.

The regiment arrived in Jacksonville on February 8. The next day at Camp Finnegan, three companies of the 8th USCT captured one prisoner and many Rebel stores. The regiment was placed on duty guarding and repairing railroad bridges at Finnegan's, Picket House, Baldwin, and Barbour's. General Gillmore met with Seymour at Jacksonville on February 14 and ordered the brigade to stay at Baldwin and not to advance without his consent. After Gillmore's departure, Seymour sent word that he intended to destroy the railroad bridge at the Suwannee River. Gillmore sent General John Turner to stop him, but thunderstorms delayed Turner by two days. The battle of Olustee occurred before Turner arrived. On February 16, Fribley expressed his disapproval of this trip to Florida in a letter to his wife: "We don't know how long we will remain here. We can't tell much about what will be done, when I am well satisfied that the head bosses are not certain as to what they want to do themselves. I have but little confidence in the show they are making. It is all show."[16] Seymour disobeyed orders, disregarded his staff's advice, and failed to heed a warning that a large Rebel force was lying in wait at Olustee.

A large number of Confederate skirmishers encountered Seymour's brigade in a swamp thirty-five miles west of Jacksonville. Henry's Mounted Brigade, the cavalry, and the 7th Connecticut went into battle first. The 7th New Hampshire was deployed to the right and the 8th USCT to the left, between artillery regiments. A few days before the battle, Seymour forced the 7th New Hampshire to exchange their Spencer carbines for unfamiliar Springfield muskets, many lacking bayonets and some inoperative. Colonel Hawley ordered the 7th New Hampshire near the Pond; however, the order was misunderstood and the regiment broke into confusion, refusing to rally. Lieutenant Oliver Norton described how the 8th USCT faced the enemy:

> Military men say it takes veteran troops to maneuver under fire, but our regiment with knapsacks on and unloaded pieces, after a run of half a mile, formed a line under the most destructive fire I ever knew. We were not more than two hundred yards from the enemy, concealed in pits and behind trees, and what did the regiment do? At first they were stunned, bewildered, and knew not what to do. They curled to the ground, and as men fell around them they seemed terribly scared, but gradually they recovered their senses and commenced firing. And here was the great trouble – they could not use their arms to advantage. We have had very little practice firing, and though they could stand and be killed, they could not kill a concealed enemy fast enough to satisfy my feelings.[17]

The 8th USCT maintained their position "before a terrible fire, closing up as their ranks were thinned out, fire in front, on their flank, and in the rear, without flinching or breaking."[18] This regiment performed "with a courage worthy of veterans."[19] Captain John Hamilton of the Third U.S. Artillery valued the sacrifice of the 8th USCT: "My heart bled for them; they fell as ten pins in a bowling alley; but everything depended on their sacrifice and that of my battery until we could be relieved or the new line formed."[20] The Confederates charged the left flank of the 8th USCT. As he ordered his men to continue firing as they slowly fell back, Fribley was shot in the chest. He told his men to carry him to the rear and died a few moments later. His body was placed on the footboard of one of Hamilton's limbers.[21] Major Burritt took command, but soon fell wounded (both legs broken). The regiment slowly retreated to the rear.

The 8th USCT carried two flags at the battle of Olustee: the national colors and the regimental flag. The sergeant carrying the regimental flag "was hit in his right hand by a ball which nearly tore off the hand. Rather than let the flag fall, the sergeant calmly seized the staff with his left hand and retained possession of the flag until he found a corporal to give the flag to for safekeeping."[22] The regimental colors were carried to the rear. Three color sergeants and five corporals of the color guard fell saving their national colors. Lieutenant Lewis carried the national colors to a battery on the left. A fragment of the regiment rallied around the flag. The horses started to the rear but soon stopped. Enemy fire forced the men to retreat, and in the confusion, the men unfortunately left the colors behind. Captain Hamilton ordered Fribley's body removed from the limber, so he could move one of his guns. "He was placed about twenty-five feet to the right and rear of my right piece, where I think he was left."[23]

Other regiments entered the battle, including the 54th Massachusetts (another black troop). The battle lasted from three o'clock p.m. until dark. The Union suffered heavy losses. The Confederates retreated at dark. The Union carried their wounded to Baldwin or Barbour. Dr. Alex. P. Heickhold, Surgeon of the 8th USCT,

> was particular in collecting the colored troops who were wounded, and placed them in his ambulance and pushed on for a place of safety. Some one thought the white troops should be brought away also; but Dr. H. said: 'I know what will become of the white troops who fall into the enemy's possession, but I am not certain as to the fate of the colored troop,' and pushed with alacrity towards Baldwin. He also dressed the wounds of all the Eighth that came into camp at Barbour, and a great many others belonging to white regiments. It looked sad to see men wounded coming into camp with their arms and equipment on, so great was their endurance and so determined were they to defend themselves to the death. I saw white troops that were not badly wounded, that had thrown away everything.[24]

General Seymour advised the Sanitary Corps to abandon the wounded; however, they continued to transport wounded to the safety of railroad cars. Confederates captured some of the wounded. A flag of truce brought news that all prisoners were being treated alike; however, Confederate regiments killed many wounded black soldiers:

> A young officer was standing in the road in front of me and I asked him, "What is the meaning of all this firing I hear going on." His reply to me

was, "Shooting niggers Sir. I have tried to make the boys desist but I can't control them." I made some answer in effect that it seemed horrible to kill the wounded devils, and he again answered, "That's so Sir, but one young fellow over yonder told me the niggers killed his brother after being wounded, at Fort Billow, and he was twenty three years old, that he had already killed nineteen and needed only four more to make the matter even, so I told him to go ahead and finis [sic] the job." I rode on but the firing continued.[25]

The 8th USCT entered this battle with twenty-one officers and 544 men, a total of 565. The regiment suffered great losses—sixty-six killed (one officer and sixty-five men), 262 wounded (wounded and missing—one officer and forty-nine men; other wounded—eight officers and 204 men), and fifteen missing men, a total loss of 343.[26] The Confederates stripped the dead of their clothing. Seymour requested the Confederates mark Fribley's grave for later reburial; however, Finegan denied his request. Seymour also requested the return of Fribley's effects to his widow. Finegan felt compassion for the widow and returned an ambrotype,[27] his watch, a letter, and Fribley's diary.[28] A letter published March 30, 1864 in the *Savannah Daily News* showed no compassion: "The black-hearted Frieble had a dog's burial. A leader of a horde of infuriated negroes, on a mission of murder, robbery and rape, ought he not have been left to rot on the plain, to the obscene birds to fatten on his vitals, and the great wolves to gnaw on his bones?"[29] Confederates probably buried Colonel Fribley in a mass grave with his men. Officers and men who survived the post-battle slaughter were imprisoned at Andersonville—stripped of their uniforms, forced to wear castoff clothing, denied medical treatment, and forced to work around the prison. "These black soldiers represented everything the South was fighting against . . . . Persons just marched them into the stockade, where they congregated in their own little encampment near the south gate—ignored by everyone, including the doctors."[30] Many of these soldiers died from their wounds.

The Olustee disaster enraged the public. Newspapers and racists denounced the black troops for running away. Seymour claimed the 54th Massachusetts was the only good black regiment under his command. As the facts became evident, it was clear that, "the African-American troops in Seymour's command, even the inexperienced Eighth USCT, acted with extraordinary heroism."[31] Seymour was blamed for disobeying orders, leading the men into a trap, and for changing the weapons of 7th New Hampshire prior to battle. He put black regiments into battle and "forgot" about them. Some blamed President Lincoln for sacrificing these men. To prevent a negative effect on black enlistments, the Congressional Committee on the Conduct of the War downplayed these stories when they investigated this battle. The Committee exonerated the president but did not blame any commander for his actions. Seymour, however, received orders to the Army of the Potomac.

The Eighth USCT fought bravely, "but the stupidity of a Commanding General is a thing that the gods themselves strive against in vain."[32] Seymour's glory seeking led to disaster for this regiment. Fribley's death was a great loss to the regiment. "Had Colonel Fribley been in command of that expedition, many dear lives might have been saved."[33] The commander of Camp William Penn,

Figure 2 "Hymn of the Freedman," by George H. Boker, 1864. http://jhir.library.jhu.edu/handle/1774.2/5689.Lithograph cover illustration of sheet music to 'Hymn of the Freedman,' depicting black soldiers of the Union 8th U.S. Colored Troops and their commanding officer, Colonel Charles W. Fribley, killed in the Battle of Olustee, Florida. Original Artwork: Lithograph by P S Duval & Son.

Louis Wagner, deserves blame for the lack of proper weapons training. Norton commented that, "Colonel Fribley had applied time and time again for permission to practice his regiment in target firing, and been always refused."[34] The regiment did not blame their colonel for their losses. They named their next principal fort outside of Jacksonville Redoubt Fribley in his honor. Today, visitors can view Fribley's name on the African American Civil War Memorial in Washington, D.C. and on the soldier's monument in the Muncy Cemetery in Pennsylvania. After the war, "the North sent 'Yankee schoolmarms' to the South to educate the newly freed slaves."[35] Kate honored Charles by becoming a "Yankee schoolmarm" in Tennessee. Pennsylvania named the GAR post (in Williamsport, Lycoming County) in his honor —Col. Chas. W. Fribley Post No. 390.

Fribley knew the risk of commanding a colored regiment— "he was actuated by the desire of aiding the emancipation of an oppressed race, and of fighting the battle of Freedom. . . . His blood has been poured out with that of his black compatriots, upon a rebellious soil. They rest together in a common grave. And when, hereafter, a grateful nation shall gather the commingled dust of these her brave defenders, no name shall be more honored than that of the gallant young soldier who believed that the cause of his country was the cause of Human Rights."[36] Although this regiment did not receive Medals of Honor for their bravery, the "wounds they bore would be the medals they would show their children and grandchildren by and by."[37] Many gave their lives for the cause of freedom.

Notes

1. George F. Linderman, *Embattled Courage: The Experience of Combat in the American Civil War* (New York: The Free Press, 1987), 7.

2. Lt. Col. Michael Lee Lanning, Ret., *The African-American Soldier: From Crispus Attucks to Colin Powell* (Secaucus, New Jersey: Carol Publishing Company, 1997), 34.

3. Ibid., 51.

4. Bernard C. Nalty, *Strength for the Fight: A History of Black Americans in the Military* (New York: The Free Press, 1986), 45.

5. Soldiers for the 7th, 8th, 9th and 10th USCT needed to be immune to tropical diseases since they would be sent to the swampy regions in the South; however, this requirement did not apply to white officers.

6. Charles Wesley Fribley, October 4, 1861, Charles Wesley Fribley diary, Manuscripts – Civil War Miscellaneous Collection, U.S. Army Military History Institute, Carlisle Barracks, Pennsylvania.

7. *The War of the Rebellion: A Compilation of the Official Records of the Union and Confederate Armies* Vol. 25/1, no. 39 (Washington: Government Printing Office, 1880), 500, reproduced in *The Civil War CD-ROM [CD-ROM]* (Carmel, Ind.: Guild Press of Indiana, 1996).

8. Charles Wesley Fribley, April 15, 1863.

9. Versalle F. Washington, *Eagles on Their Buttons: A Black Infantry Regiment in the Civil War* (Columbia: University of Missouri Press, 1999), 19.

10. Joseph T. Glatthaar, *Forged in Battle: The Civil War Alliance of Black Soldiers and White Officers* (New York: The Free Press, 1990), 48-49.

11. "Recollections of Col. Charles W. Fribley," From The October 25, 1870 and November 1, 1870 issues of the Muncy *Luminary* (transcribed by David L. Richards, Gettysburg, Pennsylvania December 6, 1994), 6.

12. Joyce Hansen, *Between Two Fires: Black Soldiers in the Civil War* (New York: Franklin Watts, 1993), 86.

13. Charles Wesley Fribley, December 25, 1863.

14. Ibid., January 7, 1864. The diary does not provide the reason for this conflict, but it may be related to Wagner not allowing the regiment to receive proper weapons training.

15. Military Service File for Charles Wesley Fribley, National Archives and Records Administration, Washington, D.C.

16. "Recollections of Col. Charles W. Fribley," 6.

17. Richard A. Sauers, *Advance the Colors!: Pennsylvania Civil War Battle Flags,* Vol. 1 (Harrisburg: Capitol Preservation Comm., 1987), 48. Oliver Norton was the bugler who helped General Butterfield write *Taps.* Norton became quartermaster for the 8th USCT.

18. William Wells Brown, *The Negro in the American Rebellion: His Heroism and His Fidelity* (New York: The Citadel Press, 1971), 218.

19. Samuel P. Bates, *History of the Pennsylvania Volunteers, 1861-5*, Vol. 10 (Wilmington, North Carolina: Broadfoot, 1993), 966.

20. *Official Records*, Vol. 53, no. 111: 25.

21. A limber is a two-wheeled horse-drawn carriage used to haul a cannon and its accessories.

22. Richard A. Sauers, 49.

23. *Official Records,* Vol. 53, no. 111: 25.

24. Edwin S. Redkey, ed., *A Grand Army of Black Men* (New York: Cambridge University Press, 1992), 42.

25. "Excerpt from the *Reminiscences of William Frederick Penniman,*" accessed 7 June 2002, http://extlab1.entnem.ufl.edu/olustee/letters/penniman.html.

26. The mascot of the 8th USCT, "Lion" – an old white dog, was wounded in the foreleg, yet he continued to be ready to march at any moment and to be first on board a vessel.

27. An ambrotype is an early photograph in which a glass negative is backed by a dark surface.

28. Fribley's 1862 diary was lost either prior to this time or was not returned to Kate.

29. William H. Nulty, *Confederate Florida: The Road to Olustee* (Tuscaloosa: The University of Alabama Press, 1990), 190. This letter also questioned the color of Fribley's wife, whether she was white or black. A photo of the couple showed they were both white.

30. William Marvel, *Andersonville: The Last Depot* (Chapel Hill: The University of North Carolina Press, 1994), 41- 43.

31. Donald Yacovone, ed., *A Voice of Thunder: The Civil War Letters of George E. Stephens* (Chicago: The University of Illinois Press, 1997), 69.

32. John McElroy, *Andersonville: A Story of Rebel Military Prisons* (New York: Fawcett Publications, 1962), 53.

33. "Recollections of Col. Charles W. Fribley," 7.

34. William H. Nulty, 143. This may have led to the conflict between Wagner and Fribley.

35. William A. Gladstone, *Men of Color* (Gettysburg: Thomas Publications, 1993), 100.

36. "Recollections of Col. Charles W. Fribley," 15.

37. Gerald F. Linderman, 32.

BIBLIOGRAPHY

DOCUMENTS AND MANUSCRIPTS
Bates, Samuel P. *History of the Pennsylvania Volunteers, 1861-5*. Wilmington,
    North Carolina: Broadfoot, 1993. Vol. 10, pp. 965-90. U.S. Army
    Military History Institute, Carlisle Barracks, Pennsylvania,
    E527B32.1993v10.

Fribley, Charles Wesley diary. U.S. Army Military History Institute Manuscripts –
    Civil War Miscellaneous Collection. [Note: Original diary is at
    USAMHI. Author has copy transcribed by David Richards, Gettysburg,
    Pennsylvania.]

Fribley family information, Max Fribley, Warsaw, Indiana.

Military Service file for Charles Wesley Fribley, National Archives and Records
    Administration, Washington, D.C.

"Recollections of Col. Charles W. Fribley." From the October 25, 1870 and
    November 1, 1870 issues of the Muncy *Luminary*. Transcribed by David
    L. Richards, Gettysburg, Pennsylvania, 6 December 1994.

Sauers, Richard A. *Advance the Colors!: Pennsylvania Civil War Battle Flags*.
    Vol. 1. Harrisburg: Capitol Preservation Committee, 1987, pp. 48-49.
    U.S. Army Military History Institute, Carlisle Barracks, Pennsylvania,
    E527.4S38.1987v1.

Taylor, Frank H. *Philadelphia in the Civil War*. Philadelphia: By the City, 1913,
    p. 191. U.S. Army Military History Institute, Carlisle Barracks,
    Pennsylvania, E527.97P54T39.

ELECTRONIC SOURCES
"An Abbreviated History of the 8th United States Colored Troops Infantry
    Regiment." Accessed 1 April 2003. http://www.angelfire.com/
    pa5/8usct/8usct_history1.html.

"The Activities at Camp William Penn." Accessed 1 April 2003. http://
    cheltenhamtownship.org/lamott/lamott1.html.

"After the Battle of Olustee, 1866 to the Present." Accessed 17 May 2002. http://
    extlab1.entnem.ufl.edu/olustee/after.html.

"Bad Rifles at Olustee." *Boston Journal*, March 4, 1864. Accessed 6 June 2002. http://extlab1.entnem.ufl.edu/olustee/letters/7thnh.html.

"The Battle of Olustee." Accessed 17 May 2002. http://extlab1.entnem.ufl.edu/olustee/battle.html.

"Report of the Battle of Olustee." *Boston Journal*, February 24, 1864. Accessed 6 June 2002. http://extlab1.entnem.ufl.edu/olustee/letters/boston-1.html.

"Capt. Loomis L. Langdon, Commanding Battery M, First Artillery, on revisiting the Battlefield." Accessed 7 June 2002. http://extlab1.entnem.ufl.edu/olustee/letters/langdon1.html.

"Civil War Books: Suggested Reading List." Accessed 4 March 2003. http://www.coax.net/people/lwf/civbooks.html.

"Colonel Charles W. Fribley: 8th U.S. Colored Troops (U.S.C.T.)." Accessed 15 May 2002. http://extlab1.entnem.ufl.edu/olustee/fribley.html.

Crowninshield, Benjamin W. "The First Regiment of Massachusetts Cavalry Volunteers in Florida." *A History of the First Regiment of Massachusetts Cavalry Volunteers.* Cambridge: Riverside Press, 1891. Accessed 7 June 2002. http://extlab1.entnem.ufl.edu/olustee/letters/mass-cav.html.

Dahl, Kathy. "Coastal War" *U.S. Civil War History and Genealogy.* Accessed 10 April 2003. http://www.genealogyforum.rootswebcom/gfaol/resource/Military/coastal.html.

"Eighth United States Colored Troops." Accessed 15 May 2002. http://extlab1.entnem.ufl.edu/olustee/8th_USCI.html.

"Eighth United States Colored Troops Unit History." Accessed 15 May 2002. http://extlab1.entnem.ufl.edu/olustee/8_US_HIS.HTML.

"Events Leading up to the Battle of Olustee." Accessed 16 May 2002. http://extlab1.entnem.ufl.edu/olustee/events.html.

Excerpt from the *Reminiscences of William Frederick Penniman (1843-1908).* Accessed 7 June 2002. http://extlab1.entnem.ufl.edu/olustee/letters/penniman.html.

"Final Report of Brig. General Joseph Finegan, commanding Confederate Forces, final report on the engagement at Olustee." Accessed 4 June 2002. http://

extlab1/entnem.ufl.edu/olustee/reports/finegan5.html.

"The Florida Expedition." *Boston Herald*, March 2, 1864. Accessed 6 June 2002. http://extlab1.entnem.ufl.edu/olustee/letters/b-herald.html.

Fox, William F. *Regimental Losses in the American Civil War (1861-1865).* Albany: Albany Publishing Company, 1889. Reproduced in *The Civil War CD-ROM.* [CD-ROM] Carmel: Guild Press of Indiana, 1997.

"GAR posts – Department of Pennsylvania." Accessed 15 April 2003. http://schooloftime.101main.com/sons/Padept/garposts.html.

"General Seymour Too Lax?" *Boston Journal*, March 10, 1864. Accessed 6 June 2002. http://extlab1.entnem.ufl.edu/olustee/letters/excuse.html.

"Letter from Captain Robert R. Newell, 54th Massachusetts," March 9, 1864. Accessed 6 June 2002. http://extlab1.entnem.ufl.edu.olustee/letters/newell01.html.

"Letter from Cpl. Henry Shackelford," February 20, 1864. Accessed 5 June 2002. http://extlab1.entnem.ufl.edu/olustee/letters/Hshackelford.html.

"Letter from H.W.B.," February 25, 1864. Accessed 6 June 2002. http://extlab1.entnem.ufl.edu/olustee/letters/hwb.html.

"Letter from Lt. Winston Stephens," February 21, 1864. Accessed 5 June 2002. http://extlab1.entnem.ufl.edu/olustee/letters/Wstephens1.html.

"Letter from Lt. Winston Stephens," February 27, 1864. Accessed 5 June 2002. http://extlab1.entnem.ufl.edu/olustee/letters/Wstephens2.html.

"Letter from Pvt. James Jordan," February 21, 1864. Accessed 5 June 2002. http://extlab1.entnem.ufl.edu/olustee/letters/Jjordan.html.

"Letters from Men of 40th Massachusetts Mounted Infantry." Accessed 6 June 2002. http://extlab1.entnem.ufl.edu/olustee/letters/40th-mass2.html.

Meginness, John F., ed. *History of Lycoming County Pennsylvania,* 1892. Accessed 15 April 2003. http://www.usgennet.org/usa/pa/county/lycoming/history/Chapter-26.html.

Norton, Oliver. "Letter from Lt. Oliver Norton, February, 1864." *Army Letter, 1861-1865.* Accessed 15 May 2002.http://extlab1.entnem.ufl.edu/olustee/

letters/onorton.html.

"Report from Brig. Gen. Jno. P. Hatch, Commanding Officer, U.S. Forces, District of Florida, on the engagement at Olustee, Florida, concerning Union wounded and dead." Accessed 4 June 2002. http://extlab1.entnem.ufl.edu/ olustee/reports/hatch.html.

"Report on Battle of Olustee." *Boston Journal*, March 2, 1864. Accessed 6 June 2002. http://extlab1.entnem.ufl.edu/olustee/letters/account.html.

"Report of Captain John Hamilton, Third U.S. Artillery, and Chief of Artillery, USA on the engagement at Olustee, Florida." Accessed 3 June 2002. http://extlab1.entnem.ufl.edu/olustee/reports/hamilton.html.

"Report of Capt. Loomis L. Langdon, Commanding Battery M, First Artillery, on the engagement at Olustee, Florida." Accessed 4 June 2002. http:// extlab1.entnem.ufl.edu/olustee/reports/langdon.html.

"Report of Lt. Andrew F. Ely, 8th United Stated [sic] Colored Troops, on the engagement at Olustee, Florida." Accessed 4 June 2002. http:// extlab1.entnem.ufl.edu/olustee/reports/A_ELY.html.

"Report of Lieutenant Frederick E. Grossman, Seventh United States Infantry, on the reburial of Union troops at Olustee, Florida." Accessed 4 June 2002. http:// extlab1.entnem.ufl.edu/olustee/reports/grossman.html.

"Report of Lt. M.B. Grant, Corps of Engineers, CSA, on the engagement at Olustee." Accessed 4 June 2002. http://extlab1.entnem.ufl.edu/olustee/ reports/grant.html.

Scott, Donald. "Camp William Penn's Black Soldiers in Blue." *America's Civil War,* November 1999. Accessed 1 April 2003. http:// preview.thehistory.net/americascivilwar/articles/1999/1199_text.html.

"Seventh New Hampshire Infantry." Accessed 30 May 2002. http:// extlab1.entnem.ufl.edu/olustee/7th_NH_inf.html.

"Soldier History: Charles W. Fribley." Accessed 7 April 2003. http:// www.civilwardata.com.

Stille, Charles J. *The History of the United States Sanitary Commission During the War of the Rebellion*, 1866. Accessed 23 April 2003. http:// www.netwalk.com/~jpr/olustee.html.

"Truman Seymour (1824-1891)." Accessed 29 May 2002. http://extlab1.entnem.ufl.edu/olustee/seymour.html.

"Union falls back on Jacksonville." *Boston Journal*, March 1, 1864. Accessed 6 June 2002. http://extlab1.entnem.ufl.edu/olustee/letters/tribute-1.html.

The War of Rebellion: A Compilation of the Official Records of the Union and Confederate Armies. Washington: Government Printing Office, 1880. Reproduced in *The Civil War CD-ROM.* [CD-ROM] Carmel: Guild Press of Indiana, 1997.

PUBLISHED WORKS

Brown, William Wells. *The Negro in the American Rebellion: His Heroism and His Fidelity*. New York: The Citadel Press, 1971.

Buckley, Gail. *American Patriots: The Story of Blacks in the Military from the Revolution to Desert Storm*. New York: Random House, 2001.

Cornish, Dudley Taylor. *The Sable Arm: Negro Troops in the Union Army, 1861-1865.* New York: W.W. Norton and Company, Inc., 1966.

Eicher, David J. *The Longest Night: A Military History of the Civil War*. New York: Simon and Schuster, 2001.

Emilio, Luis F. *A Brave Black Regiment: History of the Fifty-Fourth Regiment of Massachusetts Volunteer Infantry 1863-1865.* Salem, New Hampshire: Ayer Company Publishers, 1990.

Garrison, Web and Cheryl. *The Encyclopedia of Civil War Usage*. Nashville: Cumberland House, 2001.

Gladstone, William A. *United States Colored Troops: 1863-1867.* Gettysburg: Thomas Publications, 1990.

Glatthaar, Joseph T. *Forged in Battle: The Civil War Alliance of Black Soldiers and White Officers.* New York: The Free Press, 1990.

Gooding, Corporal James Henry. *On the Altar of Freedom: A Black Soldier's Civil War Letters From the Front*. New York: Warner Books, 1992.

Gourdin, John Raymond. *The Book of First, Last, Etcetera: Black Soldiers during the Civil War Era 1861-1867.* Columbia, Maryland: J & M Publishers,

2003.

Hansen, Joyce. *Between 2 Fires: Black Soldiers in the Civil War*. New York: Franklin Watts, 1993.

Higginson, Thomas Wentworth. *Army Life in a Black Regiment*. New York: W.W. Norton & Company, 1984.

Lanning, Lt. Col. Michael Lee (Ret.). *The African-American Soldier: From Crispus Attucks to Colin Powell*. Secaucus, New Jersey: Carol Publishing Group, 1997.

Linderman, Gerald F. *Embattled Courage: The Experience of Combat in the American Civil War*. New York: The Free Press, 1987.

McElroy, John. *Andersonville: A Story of Rebel Military Prisons*. New York: Fawcett Publications, 1962.

Marvel, William. *Andersonville: The Last Depot*. Chapel Hill: The University of North Carolina Press, 1994.

Nalty, Bernard C. *Strength for the Fight: A History of Black Americans in the Military*. New York: The Free Press, 1986.

Nulty, William H. *Confederate Florida: The Road to Olustee*. Tuscaloosa, University of Alabama Press, 1990.

Redkey, Edwins, ed. *A Grand Army of Black Men*. New York: Cambridge University Press, 1992.

Robertson, James I., Jr. *Soldiers Blue and Gray*. Columbia: University of South Carolina Press, 1998.

Schneider, Richard H. *Taps: Notes From a Nation's Heart*. New York: William Morrow, 2002.

Sneden, Robert Knox. *Eye of the Storm*. New York: The Free Press, 2000.

Washington, Versalle F. *Eagles on Their Buttons: A Black Infantry Regiment in the Civil War*. Columbia: University of Missouri Press, 1999.

Webster's New World Dictionary, 3rd College Edition. New York: Simon and Schuster, 1988.

Wilson, Joseph T. *The Black Phalanx*. Newport Beach, California: Books on Tape, 1996. (originally published in 1887).

Yacovone, Donald, ed. *A Voice of Thunder: The Civil War Letters of George E. Stephens*. Chicago: University of Illinois Press, 1997.

The Effect of Nazi Propaganda on Ordinary Germans

Judy Monhollen

Germany during the Nazi regime under Adolf Hitler contained many incredibly unique aspects, which lend to the author's desire to gain a better understanding of the actions of both the regime and ordinary Germans in the 1930s and 1940s. One of these aspects was the implementation of Hitler's racial ideology through propaganda, resulting in a number of different programs, including a hotly protested euthanasia program, sterilization programs, and, most famously, the Holocaust. Hitler highly valued propaganda as a means to reach the masses, and he did so with aplomb, founding the Reich's Ministry of Public Enlightenment and Propaganda in 1933, and placing Joseph Goebbels in charge of the Ministry.[1] Due to the extreme emphasis placed on propaganda by Hitler and Goebbels, the Nazi regime presented masterful doctrine that permeated the psyche of the German people. Nazi proselytization, including blaming the Jews for Germany's defeat in World War I, assisted in convincing the German population that the extermination of specific groups was the correct course of action to ensure the preservation of the German race.

Hitler served as a corporal in the German army during the First World War, and, in doing so, saw firsthand the horrors of trench warfare. World War I was a formative experience for Hitler and many of the Nazi Party leadership, as most fought in the war.[2] Like most German soldiers and citizens, Hitler was dismayed about the manner in which the war ended. The Treaty of Versailles named Germany as the sole aggressor in the "war-guilt" clause, Paragraph 231, forcing Germany to give up territory and pay an exorbitant amount in reparations.[3] The Nazi Party had "revolutionary" aims, and sought to create a "national" or "people's community" (*Volksgemeinschaft*), an ideal that the Nazis disseminated to all Germans in order to accomplish their goals. Because of this, the Nazi regime's propaganda aims were extraordinarily ambitious.[4] Part of the development of the new German *Volk* was finding a scapegoat for the Treaty of Versailles and the economic problems that surfaced during the Weimar Republic, including out of control inflation and mass unemployment. In Hitler's eyes, a number of culprits contributed to Germany's problems, but at the top of the list were the Jews. Hitler believed strongly that Germany suffered from a "stab-in-the-back" inflicted from within Germany by Jewish traitors and their left-wing collaborators, paying no regard to the high number of Jews who served honorably with the German army during the First World War.[5] The Nazis levied hate-filled charges against the Jews, blaming them for the devastation of the First World War, the devastating armistice in 1918, the Treaty of Versailles, the 1923 inflation, Marxism, and world communism as a whole.[6] This may seem like a great deal to place on the shoulders of one group, but Hitler did so successfully, and helped to propagate the "stab-in-the-back" myth to the German public through his propaganda program.

Hitler highly valued propaganda and the effects it could have on a population. He served as the propaganda official in the German Workers' Party prior to the development and founding of the National Socialist Party, and regarded it as the most important department.[7] As well as being a very charismatic leader in his own right, Hitler knew that propaganda was the best way to sway the masses to support his views, and was cunning in his dissemination of propaganda. Hitler was also an avid learner, believing that the best propaganda of the First World War came from the English and Americans, who dehumanized the Germans by portraying them as barbarians and Huns. In his memoir, *Mein Kampf*, Hitler consistently criticized intellectuals, and showed that he felt propaganda was effective because the masses were of limited intelligence as a whole, stating, "All propaganda must be popular and its intellectual level must be adjusted to the most limited intelligence among those it is addressed to."[8] In his aim to create a feeling of a "national community," Hitler also knew that he had to concentrate on those who were already "national-minded" to begin with, and tailor his propaganda from that point.[9] This knowledge led to anti-Semitic propaganda that focused on strengthening the national community by singling out and ostracizing those he deemed "undesirable."

Anti-Semitism was already widespread throughout Europe before the rise of Nazism, due, in part, to extreme religious views in Europe throughout the Middle Ages. Though extreme anti-Semitism waxed and waned, the European consciousness had the sentiment ingrained into their psyche. In Rothenburg ob der Tauber, a town that has a literal treasure trove of medieval architecture and a long and proud history, the citizens still harbored strong anti-Semitic sentiment. In the Middle Ages, Rothenburg, like most of Europe, victimized Jews through repeated persecution and pogroms, resulting in the complete expulsion of its Jewish community in 1520. Rothenburg also barred Jews from returning until after German unification in 1871, when Jews received full citizenship.[10] The citizens and leaders of Rothenburg were proud of this achievement, and assisted in the transformation of the town from a normal German town to an ideal Nazi community. Anti-Semitic propaganda was widespread in Rothenburg, as it was a popular tourist destination for the Nazi *Kraft durch Freude* (Strength through Joy) workers' program designed to garner support for the Nazi party from laborers by providing benefits like paid vacations to various tourist spots in Europe.[11] On the gates of the town, plaques emblazoned with anti-Semitic slogans reasserted the strong local history of a German community's struggle against Jewish intrigues, and tourists could buy these images on postcards.[12] Though not directed by the Reich's Ministry of Propaganda, this was still an effective form of propaganda. These postcards, though seen as tourist fare, undoubtedly carried anti-Semitic messages, however subtle, to many of the tourists' family and friends both in Germany and abroad. Because of the extreme anti-Semitism present in Rothenburg, by October 24, 1938, all of Rothenburg's Jews relocated elsewhere, due to a night of supposedly spontaneous mob vandalism and violence. The town's leaders framed the expulsion of the Jews in historical terms, hearkening back to their medieval roots.[13] Rothenburg's history provided an ideal framework for Hitler to build on in creating an ideal Nazi community; one that the Nazis attempted to imitate to supplement propaganda that called for Germans to come together as one large idyllic German community, stressing the glory of Germany and the "master race."

The idealism of Rothenburg's manufactured Nazi community reflected Nazi propaganda, stressing the transcendence of social and class divisiveness through a new ethnic unity based on "true" German values.[14] The Nazis recognized that propaganda had to reinforce values and prejudices that already existed within the German community. Manufacturing a new value system created friction, and undermined the Nazi regime's efforts in creating a perfect *Volksgemeinschaft* (peoples' community).[15] By playing on preexisting values and prejudices, there was a better chance of achieving a consensus in thought because the people already held those thoughts, though not to the extreme that Nazism required. Because the Nazis attempted to reflect the roots and antecedents of *völkisch* thought, they focused on four major themes. First, was to appeal to national unity based on the principle of "community before the individual." This was important to further the agenda of a sense of social responsibility to every German rather than focusing on one's own needs. Second, was the need for racial purity. Jews, as well as other ethnic groups, "tainted" the purity of the German race, and thus were a detriment to German society in the eyes of the Nazis. By stressing racial purity, German citizens would grow in their national identity, and support the ideal of the "national community." Third, was a hatred of enemies, which increasingly centered on Jews and Bolsheviks. The Nazis felt that Jews, in particular, were a conniving race who would stop at nothing to achieve world domination, and would crush any in their path. This idea also tied into the "stab-in-the-back" myth surrounding the Treaty of Versailles. If Jews and Bolsheviks were the cause of Germany's demise during World War I, there was no stopping them from completely destroying German society. Finally, Nazi propaganda should hinge on charismatic leadership, or *Führerprinzip*. Hitler recognized the value of charisma in leading a people, and chose charismatic individuals to lead in the different *Gaus*, or regions, in Germany. Leaders with excellent public speaking skills could enthrall and excite a crowd, which in turn had the ability to enhance the importance of community. Overall, the central goal of Nazi propaganda was to restructure German society so the prevailing class, religious, and sectional loyalties would be replaced by a new and heightened national awareness, creating the ideal national community.[17] Therefore, the focus on anti-Semitic propaganda played an important role in creating this new national awareness, as the number of voters who were not anti-Semitic was not so large as to deny the Nazis their required level of national support.[18]

The virulent anti-Semitism that seemed to pervade the national consciousness did not really build steam until after the Nazi Party successfully gained a wide voter base. Though anti-Semitism and elimination of the Jews was never really a primary goal of Hitler or the Nazi Party, the racial ideology of the Nazi regime has come to the forefront due to the resulting Holocaust. There has been much debate on the responses of German citizens as well as the actions of the Germans concerning the killing of approximately six million Jews, mostly in speculation of how a civilized nation could have overlooked killing on such a massive scale. In order to understand how the Nazi regime was able to justify various pogroms and violence towards the Jews, it is important to understand the history of anti-Semitism in Europe. As mentioned in the case of Rothenburg, anti-Semitism was very prevalent in all areas of Europe, as has been confirmed by many reputable historians on the subject.[19] When one considers the long reach of the Catholic Church throughout Europe's history, this should come as no surprise. Alfons Heck, in his book *A Child of Hitler: Germany in the Days When God Wore a Swastika*, states, "All Catholic children knew that the Jews had killed Christ."[20] This has long been a key belief in Catholicism, and Martin Luther carried this belief forward into Protestantism. As the Protestant Reformation gained support, Martin Luther felt that the Jews would convert to Protestantism, and when they did not, he wrote a number of extremely virulent anti-Semitic treatises, including *The Jews and Their Lies* written in 1543.[21] In the days when the church was the center of the community, these prejudices firmly sunk their claws into the European consciousness. Even if prejudices against Jews were not necessarily overt, they nonetheless existed in the collective European subconscious through the teachings of the Church. While there were definite anti-Semitic undertones through religious channels, anti-Semitism did not take on a religious tone in Hitler's mind, as he saw them as a specific race; even Jews who converted to Christianity could not be trusted.[22]

In the 1800s, a number of anti-Semitic political theorists and philosophers helped to further ingrain anti-Semitic sentiments into the population. This is when some of the metaphors describing Jews as a pestilence took root. One anti-Semitic political theorist, Paul Anton de Lagarde, stated, "One does not have dealings with pests and parasites; one does not rear and cherish them; one destroys them as speedily and thoroughly as possible."[23] In fact, one of the most widespread slogans used by Nazi propagandists was, *"Die Juden sind unser Unglück,"* or, "The Jews are Our Misfortune." The Nazis used this slogan on banners at Nazi rally parties, as well as on posters in the streets.[24] The fact that anti-Semitism was so widespread before the Nazis came into power was certainly a contributing factor in the European community's apathy towards anti-Jewish policies that eventually led to the Holocaust.

Control over Nazi propaganda was tight and disseminated in very specific ways. Early on, the Ministry of Public Enlightenment and Propaganda took over print media in an attempt to control the release of news to the public. As early as 1931, the *Munich Post* reported that it knew of a secret Nazi plan to deprive Jews of civil rights, confiscate their property, and achieve the "Final Solution" for the "Jewish Question" by removing Jews from German society through slave labor.[25] Clearly, the Nazi regime did not accept these types of stories. In 1926, Joseph

Goebbels founded *Der Angriff* (The Attack), a Berlin newspaper and organ of the Nazi Party that helped to incite violence against German Jews. Julius Streicher, the editor and publisher of *Der Stürmer* (The Attacker), played on fears by reviving the medieval accusations that Jews murdered Christian children and used their blood for perverted religious rituals.[26] Of course, these types of accusations were permissible, and often encouraged. The Ministry of Public Enlightenment and Propaganda quickly took control of newspaper censorship. Each morning, the editors of the Berlin daily newspapers and the correspondents of those published elsewhere in the Reich gathered at the Ministry. Goebbels or one of his aides dictated what news to print and suppress, how to write the news and headline it, what campaigns to call off or institute, and the desired editorials for the day.[27] All foreign news had to come from the German Press Agency, the ministry determined which press conferences journalists could attend, and provided complete articles for the newspapers to use.[28] By controlling print media, the Nazis had an incredible advantage when deportations and exterminations began. The Ministry of Propaganda was able to black out all facts or information relating to deportation or extermination, as well as other types of persecution that would have led to any questioning of Nazi policies.[29] In addition to formal censorship positions, the Nazis also ensured that local press would not oppose them through the creation of a system of terror. Those newspaper editors who opposed the policies of the Nazi regime had to look over their shoulders for the Gestapo. Despite the critical importance of controlling mass media, newspapers were not the only Nazi method of garnering support. Mass demonstrations were an important tool to gain support from the general population.[30]

Mass demonstrations were a hallmark of the Nazi regime. There were many advantages to these public meetings, as they drew large crowds and developed an air of excitement among the spectators that was unmatched by any other form of propaganda. Public marches were very common, and ritualistically submerged all individuality. These marches were a publicly visible community of indistinguishable human beings ordered by a will that was exterior to themselves, and a perfect visualization of the Nazi goal of establishing a tight-knit national community.[31] Hitler felt that mass meetings were crucial in developing *esprit de corps*, and felt they were necessary to help individuals overcome an innate fear of being alone. In watching a mass meeting, that individual gets the picture of the larger community that they have entered, thus strengthening and encouraging them.[32] Mass meetings were also a straightforward way to direct propaganda to the masses and in doing so appeal to emotions rather than reason.[33] Crowds are easier to incite than individuals are, and Hitler was well aware of this phenomenon, so he took advantage of appealing to crowds as often as possible. In Northeim, Germany, the Nazis designed mass demonstrations to convince Northeimers that they were entering into a new era.[34] Alfons Heck also recounts a time when Hitler came through his small town of Wittlich in the Mosel Valley of the Rhine. Heck claims that the town was ecstatic because Hitler symbolized the promise of a new Germany, and a proud Reich that had found its rightful place.[35] Nuremberg became the center of the Nazi universe for a week each September when the Nazis came to put on massive parades to exhibit the solidarity of the German people.[36] Mass meetings were highly choreographed events, and the propaganda department from each *Gau* ensured speakers and topics were in tune with local conditions and economic circumstances in an effort to ensure support.[37] The focus of mass demonstrations was to garner public support for Nazi policies, but they also disseminated anti-Semitic propaganda throughout Germany via public meetings to support anti-Jewish policies as well as euthanasia and sterilization programs. The Nazis spread anti-Semitic propaganda throughout many different areas, quickly indoctrinating the schools to target Germany's youth.

The Nazis quickly discovered that one portion of the population that was particularly receptive to the notion of a "national community" was the German youth. Because of this, the Nazis moved quickly to teach service and obedience, stamping out the individualism and enthusiasm of German youth by instilling a sense of belonging to an exclusive racial community.[38] The move to convert schools into centers of Nazi ideology was surprisingly easy, as most teachers were already hostile to the Weimar Republic, and already sympathetic to the Nazis. In fact, they were overrepresented in the Nazi Party with thirty-six percent of teachers belonging to the Nazi Party by 1936. In 1933, the Nazis purged all Communist, Socialist, and Jewish teachers, and proceeded to restructure the curriculum to spread their propaganda to children.[39] History classes focused on the Nazi revolution and reinterpreted history based on racial principles, especially the significance of the Aryan race in world history. Biology centered on the laws of heredity, racial breeding, and the need for racial purity.[40] In addition, many children's books of the time had overtly anti-Semitic tones. The anti-Semitic book *Der Giftpilz* (The Poisonous Mushroom) highlighted the medieval theme of the

Jews as the killers of Christ. A line from the book urges children, "When you see a cross, then think of the horrible murder by the Jews on Golgotha."[41] Another book titled *Trau Keinem Fuchs auf greener Heid und Keinem Jud bei Seinem Eid* (You Can't Trust a Fox in a Heath and a Jew on His Oath) helped in disseminating anti-Semitic propaganda to the unsuspecting German youth.[42] Though targeting children is undoubtedly a harsh manner in which to further a propaganda campaign, the Nazis felt it was important to indoctrinate the youth because they were the future of the Reich. Children were also uncommonly cruel, desensitized by Nazi rhetoric, and were quick to turn on their Jewish counterparts.[43] Alfons Heck makes an interesting observation when he states, "Even in working democracies, children are too immature to question the veracity of what they are taught by their educators."[44] When one thinks about this statement, it is incredibly accurate. Parents teach their children from an early age to listen to their teachers. As a result, children perceive nearly everything a teacher says as fact. This method was so effective that the Nazis used it to encourage children to denounce parents who were hostile to the Nazi Party.[45]

In addition to infiltrating the German education system, the Nazi Party set up a number of different clubs and organizations for children to join. The most well-known was the Hitler Youth, and many young boys aspired to be a part of such a tight-knit organization. Like documented "gang" mentality, the Hitler Youth gave young men a place where they felt like they were a part of an exclusive community. Alfons Heck aspired to be a part of the Hitler Youth, and firmly believed in the two tenets of the Nazi creed: belief in the innate superiority of the Germanic-Nordic race, and the conviction that total submission to the welfare of the state—personified by the *Führer*—was his first duty.[46] The Hitler Youth were highly visible and marched with military units in public demonstrations, giving young men a sense that they wanted to belong to this group. Girls were also able to join Nazi groups, but learned from an early age that their goal in life was to grow up to be prolific mothers.[47] The Nazi Party felt it was incredibly important to indoctrinate children early, as they were central to the ideal of the thousand-year Reich.

While German parents were not widely opposed to the indoctrination of schools, the Nazi policy of weeding out people, including children, who were considered "mentally handicapped," drew loud protests. A sterilization program initiated by the Nazi regime did not get very far through legal means. In an attempt to purify the German race, the Nazis attempted to start a sterilization program, and a target of this program was children deemed "mentally deficient." The Nazis gave instructors in schools guidelines on how to explain to parents the importance of sterilizing their child. Teachers told parents that sterilization of their child was a "necessary offering to the altar of the Fatherland."[48] These instructors received instruction to stress that the law is a "blessing for the child to be sterilized as well as for the parents and the entire family, for the unborn generation, and for the entire national community," as well.[49] This program encountered stiff opposition, but the program still carried on in a more discreet manner.

Another program that received a great deal of criticism was the euthanasia program. The Nazis designed this program to eradicate members of German society that could not provide a meaningful contribution to the German community. The Nazis created propaganda to support this program, and claimed that the money it took to feed, house, and clothe one disabled person for a single day could help an entire German family to survive for a year. This propaganda helped to prepare the German people for the murder of those deemed genetically inferior.[50] However, the euthanasia program drew very public protests, mostly from Germany's Catholic and Lutheran leaders. Widespread protests forced the Nazis to halt operations on August 24, 1941, but they continued to kill secretly.[51] Though the euthanasia program encountered fervent opposition, the anti-Semitic policies leading to the Holocaust did not draw protests at the same level.

When the Nuremberg Laws were set in place to limit the civil rights of Jews in Germany, there was almost no protest, but it also helped to increase anti-Semitic sentiments because it affected non-Jews. Now it was essential for German citizens to prove their "Aryan" ancestry, and the task of certifying people's Aryan identities soon fell on priests and pastors, clerks, and archivists.[52] It is difficult to determine the public opinion on these policies, mostly because the Gestapo effectively squashed all public opposition, but one event that affected the German public was *Kristallnacht*, or the "Night of Broken Glass," which took place on the night of November 9-10, 1938. Joseph Goebbels and several other top party officials encouraged and even directed this event as part of an escalating campaign of anti-Semitic violence.[53] Despite dehumanizing propaganda, the German public witnessed *Kristallnacht*, making it impossible to deny the violence directed towards German Jews. Many Germans were privately appalled at the violence displayed on *Kristallnacht*, but few publicly spoke out against the occurrence.[54]

Many felt that the violence unleashed was unnecessary, but by then, the all-pervasive fear of the Gestapo had taken hold, so most Germans were unwilling to speak out against the violence due to a sense of self-preservation. Despite the disgust felt at the outcome of *Kristallnacht*, when the mass resettlement of the Jews began, most Germans were silent, making it difficult to determine whether they knew what Hitler's plans were for the "Final Solution."

The sheer amount of anti-Semitic propaganda distributed throughout Germany had an incredible effect on the German people. Though most Germans were not fervently anti-Semitic, this propaganda still invaded their subconscious to the point where they simply did not care about the fate of their Jewish neighbors. Already mentioned was the history of anti-Semitism throughout Europe. The latent anti-Semitism, which already existed in the collective minds of the German citizens, had a sad result on the implementation of Hitler's "Final Solution." The years immediately after World War I had a profound effect on the German people as a whole. Many Germans were already disgusted with the outcome of the Treaty of Versailles and the economic troubles that plagued them during the interwar years, and Nazi propaganda played up the myth of Jewish involvement that resulted in Germany's troubles. Because of this, the German people were already susceptible to Nazi propaganda due to a deep sense of national humiliation and frustration at economic problems.[55] No political party demonstratively defended Jewish interests, and the widespread acts of violence against Jews even in the Weimar period point to a very broad tolerance to anti-Semitism at the very least.[56]

Actions such as the boycott on Jewish businesses and the banishment of Jews from the legal and government professions actually garnered a large amount of support for the Nazis, particularly from business owners. Boycotting Jewish shops meant more business for German shop owners. Ejecting Jewish lawyers from courts meant more business for Christian lawyers. In addition, dismissing Jews from government jobs meant more posts available for non-Jewish Germans. Each action showed willingness among non-Jewish Germans to profit from racial and anti-Semitic prejudice.[57] Very few were willing to stick up for their Jewish neighbors, and this was largely due to Nazi tactics of violence and intimidation.[58] The climate of fear helped to perpetrate the increased violence against Jews by the Nazi Party, paving the way for the mass extermination of the Jews in the Holocaust.

In addition to fear tactics employed by the Nazis, the virulent propaganda portrayed the Jewish people as a race bent on world domination. Propaganda about the evils of race defilement helped to poison relationships between Aryans and Jews. As such, Germans avoided all contacts that suggested traitorous association with the enemies of Aryan blood.[59] Filmstrips portrayed Jews as racial "bastards."[60] In addition, Nazi euphemisms for Jews included words such as "vermin" and "pestilence," which helped in further dehumanizing the Jewish people.[61] Christopher Browning, in examining how a group of reserve police officers could coldheartedly kill thousands of Jews, mentions a quote by John Dower from the book *War Without Mercy* which states, "The Dehumanization of the Other contributed immeasurably to the psychological distancing that facilitated killing."[62] This statement also holds true for the general public. By dehumanizing the Jewish people, the public learned to turn a blind eye to the fate of German Jews.

Germans who lived through the period of the Holocaust have said that they had no concept of the extent of killing that occurred under the Nazi regime. Recent studies have brought new evidence to light showing that news of mass shootings and extermination camps came from the East, but Germans simply did not discuss this news. In a speech to SS officers, Heinrich Himmler openly discussed the evacuation of the Jews to various camps. Himmler stressed the importance of duty to the German people, and tried to ease the psychological damage of killing by arguing that killing a few now would save tens of thousands of German lives later. When speaking of the evacuation of the Jews, Himmler stated, "Among ourselves, this once, it shall be uttered quite frankly; but in public we will never speak of it."[63] This statement implies a certain amount of secrecy concerning the evacuation of the Jews. It seems clear that the Nazis at least knew what they were doing could be construed badly by the public, and attempted to ensure that the public would not discover the true implementation of Hitler's "Final Solution." The Nazis tried to be in tune with the mood and bearing of the German people, and gave extensive reports on the subject. Because of this, it is clear that the attitudes and behavior of "ordinary" Germans were far from uniform on a whole range of issues.[64] Overall, it seems as though there was simply a lack of interest in the fate of the Jews in Europe. It is impossible to determine the number of Germans who knew directly about the extermination of the Jews, and what degree of knowledge they possessed. However, there were most certainly widespread rumors in circulation about the fate of the Jews, and the information contained in the rumors were explicit enough to indicate that there were a great number of Jews being killed in the east.[65] Hitler referred to these rumors in an attempt to counter them, as did Martin Bormann. Letters from the front even described mass shootings, one of which detailed the shooting of 30,000 Jews in one town.[66] Therefore, evidence shows that information pointing to genocidal policies was widely available in Germany and not contained to a tiny minority of the population.[67]

In light of this evidence, why did the German public choose to ignore the rumors and stand silent? It is possible that many who heard these rumors felt they were simply too outrageous to be true. It is often difficult for humans, as a whole, to grasp the killing of hundreds of thousands of human beings even if one knows the exact number. It is also possible that the years of propaganda effectively dehumanized the Jews to the point where German simply dismissed the rumors as wartime casualties, and, "terrible things happen in war."[68] Widespread knowledge of shootings met with a number of responses—from overt approval to blank disapproval—but most Germans were apathetic, felt powerless to do anything about it, or turned a blind eye to the horrible truth.[69] Apathy seemed to be the most common reaction, and corresponded to the latent anti-Semitism that had permeated European society since the Middle Ages. One should also consider the need for self-preservation. The Nazis built their regime on fear and intimidation, and in this type of climate, Germans were more concerned with ensuring their individual safety than worrying about events happening in Poland or Russia where the killing of the majority of Jews occurred.[70] The Nazis imprisoned those Germans who did come forward to oppose publicly the shooting and gassing of Jews, so it is no wonder that most Germans tended to mind their own business and learned how to *not* learn about the number of Jews being slaughtered in the east.[71]

In the end, it is clear that the German public did know a great deal about the fate of the Jews, and did nothing to prevent it. There is no doubt that propaganda played a large part in reviving anti-Semitic sentiments from the Middle Ages, in addition to creating a climate of fear where German citizens did not feel it was prudent to stick up for their Jewish neighbors. Though some resistance groups surfaced, mostly against the regime, they were few and far between, and, thus, largely ineffective. Daniel Jonah Goldhagen has blamed the entire German population for the Holocaust by stating that they formed the assenting majority and created pressure for dissenting individuals, making them all party to the killing that occurred in the Holocaust,[72] but this is an oversimplification and patently untrue. While there were certainly many who were apathetic to the fate of the Jews, there is no evidence to support the assertion that all Germans would have supported genocide on the scale of the Holocaust. There were certainly those who worked the system to their advantage, but most felt powerless to do anything, and the killing of Jews was not an immediate concern. Many who denied the existence of the camps received a nasty dose of reality when the Allied forces discovered them. The Allies declared martial law, and, in many cases, forced local German civilians to personally confront the crimes committed by their countrymen in helping to bury the dead and clean up the camps.[73] However, there is no doubt that propaganda played an important role in dehumanizing the Jewish people, and integrating the German people into a "national community." The testimony of most of the defendants in the war crimes trial at Nuremberg generally used two base arguments: that they knew nothing about the murder of the Jews and that they were only obeying orders.[74] These answers have great implications on the effect of propaganda on the whole of German society.

Notes

1. Jeremy Noakes, "Leaders of the People? The Nazi Party and German Society," *Journal of Contemporary History* 39, no. 2 (April 2004): 190.

2. Ibid., 198.

3. Richard Bessel, "The Nazi Capture of Power," *Journal of Contemporary History* 39, no. 2 (April 2004): 173.

4. David Welch, "Propaganda and the Volksgemeinschaft: Constructing a People's Community," *Journal of Contemporary History* 39, no. 2 (April 2004): 213.

5. Louis Weber, comp., *The Holocaust Chronicle* (Lincolnwood, Illinois: Legacy Publishing, 2009), 21.

6. Hermann Beck, "Between the Dictates of Conscience and Political Expediency: Hitler's Conservative Alliance Partner and Antisemitism during the Nazi Seizure of Power," *Journal of Contemporary History* 41, no. 4 (October 2006): 611.

7. Adolf Hitler, *Mein Kampf*, trans. Ralph Mannheim (Boston: Houghton Mifflin Company, 1971), 579.

8. Ibid., 180.

9. Ibid., 343.

10. Joshua Hagen, "The Most German of Towns: Creating an Ideal Nazi Community in Rothenburg ob der Tauber," *Annals of the Association of American Geographers* 94, no. 1 (March 2004): 219-220.

11. Ibid., 209.

12. Ibid., 220.

13. Ibid., 221.

14. Welch, 213.

15. Ibid., 216.

16. Ibid., 217.

17. Ibid., 217.

18. Bessel, 170.

19. Mention of widespread anti-Semitism in Europe is mentioned by historians such as Joshua Hagen, Richard Bessel, Daniel Jonah Goldhagen, and Laurence Rees, among others.

20. Alfons Heck, *A Child of Hitler: Germany in the Days When God Wore a Swastika* (Phoenix: Renaissance House, 1985), 14.

21. Jackson J. Spielvogel, *Hitler and Nazi Germany,* Fifth Edition (Upper Saddle Creek, New Jersey: Pierson Prentice Hall, 2005), 272.

22. Weber, 42.

23. Ibid., 32.

24. Ibid., 18.

25. Ibid., 26.

26. Ibid., 79.

27. William L. Shirer, *The Rise and Fall of the Third Reich* (New York: Fawcett Crest, 1960), 338.

28. Spielvogel, 157.

29. Allan Mitchell, ed., *The Nazi Revolution: Hitler's Dictatorship and the German Nation,* Fourth Edition (Boston: Houghton Mifflin Company, 1997), 192.

30. William Sheridan Allen, *The Nazi Seizure of Power: The Experience of a Single German Town, 1922-1945* (New York: Franklin Watts, 1984), 206.

31. Gerhard L. Weinberg, *Germany, Hitler & World War II* (New York: Cambridge University Press, 1995), 62.

32. Hitler, 478.

33. Richard J. Evans, *The Coming of the Third Reich* (New York: Penguin Books, 2003), 168.

34. Allen, 208.

35. Heck, 2.

36. Weber, 117.

37. Benjamin Sax and Dieter Kuntz, comps., *Inside Hitler's Germany: A Documentary History of Life in the Third Reich* (Lexington, Massachusetts: D.C. Heath and Company, 1992), 99.

38. Welch, 230.

39. Spielvogel, 173.

40. Ibid., 175.

41. Weber, 77.

42. Ibid., 100.

43. Ibid., 94.

44. Heck, 3.

45. Welch, 233.

46. Heck, 8.

47. Weber, 82.

48. Sax and Kuntz, 211.

49. Ibid., 213.

50. Weber, 93.

51. Ibid., 169.

52. Ibid., 55.

53. Hagen, 221-222.

54. Weber, 143.

55. Ibid., 217.

56. Bessel, 171.

57. Ibid., 178.

58. Ibid., 180.

59. Weber, 94.

60. Ibid., 107.

61. Ibid., 215.

62. Christopher R. Browning, *Ordinary Men: Reserve Police Battalion 101 and the Final Solution in Poland* (New York: Harper Perennial, 1998), 162.

63. Russell J. Barber, Lanny B. Fields, and Cheryl A. Riggs, eds., *Reading the Global Past: Volume Two 1500 to the Present* (Boston: Bedford Books, 1998), 146.

64. Ian Kershaw, *Hitler, the Germans, and the Final Solution* (New Haven, Connecticut: Yale University Press, 2008), 140.

65. Kershaw, 141.

66. Ibid., 144.

67. Ibid., 142.

68. Ibid., 145-146.

69. Ibid., 147.

70. Ibid., 148.

71. Ibid., 203.

72. Daniel Jonah Goldhagen, *Hitler's Willing Executioners: Ordinary Germans and the Holocaust* (New York: Vantage Books, 1997), 417.

73. Weber, 595.

74. Spielvogel, 306.

BIBLIOGRAPHY

Allen, William Sheridan. *The Nazi Seizure of Power: The Experience of a Single German Town, 1922-1945*. New York: Franklin Watts, 1984.

Barber, Russell J., Lanny B. Fields, and Cheryl A. Riggs, eds. *Reading the Global Past: Volume Two 1500 to the Present*. Boston: Bedford Books, 1998.

Bessel, Richard. "The Nazi Capture of Power." *Journal of Contemporary History* 39, no. 2 (April 2004): 169-188.

Browning, Christopher R. *Ordinary Men: Reserve Police Battalion 101 and the Final Solution in Poland*. New York: Harper Perennial, 1998.

Evans, Richard J. *The Coming of the Third Reich*. New York: Penguin Books, 2003.

Goldhagen, Daniel Jonah. *Hitler's Willing Executioners: Ordinary Germans and the Holocaust*. New York: Vantage Books, 1997.

Hagen, Joshua. "The Most German of Towns: Creating an Ideal Nazi Community in Rothenburg ob der Tauber." *Annals of the Association of American Geographers* 94, no. 1 (March 2004): 207-227.

Heck, Alfons. *A Child of Hitler: Germany in the Days When God Wore a Swastika*. Phoenix: Renaissance House, 1985.

Hitler, Adolf. *Mein Kampf*. Translated by Ralph Mannheim. Boston: Houghton Mifflin Company, 1971.

Kershaw, Ian. *Hitler, the Germans, and the Final Solution*. New Haven, Connecticut: Yale University Press, 2008.

Mitchell, Allan, ed. *The Nazi Revolution: Hitler's Dictatorship and the German Nation,* Fourth Edition. Boston: Houghton Mifflin Company, 1997.

Noakes, Jeremy. "Leaders of the People? The Nazi Party and German Society." *Journal of Contemporary History* 39, no. 2 (April 2004): 189-212.

Rees, Laurence. *Auschwitz: A New History*. New York: Public Affairs, 2005.

Sax, Benjamin and Dieter Kuntz, comps. *Inside Hitler's Germany: A Documentary History of Life in the Third Reich*. Lexington, Massachusetts: D.C. Heath and Company, 1992.

Shirer, William L. *The Rise and Fall of the Third Reich*. New York: Fawcett Crest, 1960.

Spielvogel, Jackson J. *Hitler and Nazi Germany,* Fifth Edition. Upper Saddle River, New Jersey: Pierson Prentice Hall, 2005.

Weber, Louis, comp. *The Holocaust Chronicle*. Lincolnwood, Illinois: Legacy Publishing, 2009.

Weinberg, Gerhard L. *Germany, Hitler & World War II*. New York: Cambridge University Press, 1995.

Welch, David. "Propaganda and the Volksgemeinschaft: Constructing a People's Community." *Journal of Contemporary History* 39, no. 2 (April 2004): 213-238.

Traditionalist, Centrist, and Revisionist Schools: The Controversy and Debate over the "Great Nanking Massacre"

Alice L. (Parker) Alvarado

> I have had to look at so many corpses over the last few weeks that I can keep my nerves in check even when viewing these horrible cases. It really doesn't leave you in a 'Christmas' mood; but I wanted to see these atrocities with my own eyes so that I can speak as an eyewitness later. A man cannot be silent about this kind of cruelty!
>
> —John Rabe

In December of 1937, the Japanese Imperial Army marched into China and began committing acts of aggression upon the lay citizens that many would deem "atrocities." Eyewitness accounts, diaries, letters, and photographs captured unthinkable crimes against countless men, women, and children. Rape, murder, arson, and looting were rampant, and the city of Nanking became a symbol, to some, of "one of the worst instances of mass extermination."[1] In the 1970s, a debate began over the actual destruction inflicted upon the citizens of Nanking and other cities. The event received many labels from "The Rape of Nanking" and "The Great Nanking Massacre," to the "Nanking Incident" and the "Nanking Campaign," all of which would be important to certain schools of thought that would emerge on the subject.

This essay will seek to explore and explain differing schools of thought, as the "Rape of Nanking" is not a cut and dry issue even some seventy years later. Journalists, historians, scholars, and regular citizens will all disagree on the matter to some extent. Some of the major factions that emerged, and which the author will examine, are the Traditionalists, the Centrists, and the Revisionists. The author will also mention some minor factions as they pertain to the major factions and will investigate other issues such as the timeline argument, and the numbers argument.

The search for objectivity among extreme (and not so extreme) schools of thought will begin with works by investigative journalists, which include newspaper and magazine articles. Eyewitness accounts and family stories passed down from generations receive significant weight when dealing with the subject.

Original research by scholars in Japan, China, and the United States fueled the debate further as the questions "did it really happen" and "why did it happen" force themselves to the forefront.

The Traditionalists

In 1971, a Japanese reporter by the name of Honda Katsuichi traveled to China on an investigative reporting mission, and reported his findings back to *Asahi*, the newspaper for which he worked.[2] He wrote a series of articles he then converted into a book that detailed enormous atrocities committed by the Japanese Imperial Army on the Chinese people in 1937. In his mind, and according to his evidence, the Rape of Nanking did take place; it was absolutely illegal, countless women and girls were raped, and as many as 300,000 plus people were slaughtered during that period. With the advent of Honda's writings came an analysis by the scholar Hora Tomio who began the Traditionalist school of thought.[3] They both believed wholeheartedly in the findings of the International Military Tribunal for the Far East (IMFTE, 1946-48) which executed two high-ranking Japanese military officers for war crimes.[4] Honda came to be known as a Traditionalist, taking a position which has also been called "The Avowal Faction," "The Atrocities School," or the "Massacre School." Scholars considered Honda an "Extreme Traditionalist" while they considered Hora Tomio a "Moderate Traditionalist."[5] What differed between the two was their belief in the number of people murdered.[6] According to Yamamoto, Honda was instrumental in researching and discovering primary sources such as letters and diaries, but his goal was to disprove revisionist opinions.[7] Did Honda have personal motives in wanting to prove his own theory rather than simply to obtain the truth?

According to Gamble and Watanabe, some of his countrymen hated Honda for "outing" the atrocities of the war, but he was "dedicated to revealing the historical truth, no matter how painful or personally risky it may prove to be."[8] On the other hand, some felt "Honda's attitude seemed cavalier to many Japanese—not all of them closet chauvinists—who felt that journalists should get their facts and figures straight and present both sides of the story."[9] Those who came to that conclusion did so by analyzing the "100 man killing contest." According to the story, two Japanese soldiers by the names of Mukai and Noda had a contest to see who would be the first to kill one hundred Chinese. Both were neck in neck in the

90

race, and at the end, Mukai had killed 107 and Noda had killed 105. Neither soldier could say who killed 100 first, so they kept going until they reached 150.[10] Hora first analyzed this story when he read it in a book published in 1966 by Omori Minoru.[11] Since then, one cannot research this topic without reading about this "contest" in nearly every publication on the matter. Traditionalists tended to take the view that this story was fact, but later evidence showed that writers may have exaggerated the story and they had to admit that this particular story was not "as they first depicted it."[12] Although the Traditionalist school can be broken into sub-factions, they all tend to agree on the guilt of the Japanese Imperial Army.

The Centrists

The second school of thought on the issue of Nanking is the Centrists, also known as "Minimalists." Centrists are a group that cannot seem to commit to either side of the argument and they remain in-between. They are "those who criticize or are criticized by both the revisionists and the traditionalists."[13] They take heat from both sides for being neutral, and believe that each school has a "political position toward China and other Asian countries."[14] Kitamura argued that he deemed even the best-intentioned historians to be Centrists when they tried to be objective in their work on the subject. He said that researchers on the subject always take a certain "political position" and naysayers always believe a motive is involved.[15] For example, if he gave evidence of an atrocity, one school may agree with him and the other attacks him as being a part of that school. If he presented evidence leaning toward the other group, the opposite group attacks him again. Since he is a Japanese citizen, they accuse him of not being able to be objective on the subject, and therefore, he must take the approach of an historian and "return to the basics of historiographic research" in order for them to take him remotely seriously.[16]

Centrists can be broken into the sub-categories of Traditionalist Centrists and Revisionist Centrists. Both groups believe in the same basic principles; the Japanese soldiers participated in wretched behavior, they executed POWs and it was illegal, but the massacre of innocent civilians did not occur. The only aspect that set the two groups apart, like the Traditionalists, were the numbers of people actually murdered.[17]

The Revisionists

The Revisionist group was an interesting school of thought that was conceived and slowly evolved, through evidence, into something completely different. Scholars called the Revisionist camp the "Illusion" faction or the "Denial" group. Certain authors, appalled at the slander of the Japanese Army, government, and way of life, at first, flat out denied that the Rape of Nanking ever occurred. Tanaka Masaasi wrote *Fabrication of the Nanking Massacre* in 1984 that contended that all documents and photos of the event were "faked" and he placed blame for the war on China.[18] Yamamoto Shichihei, who was previously an army officer, wrote under the pen name of Isaiah Ben-Dasan and began to raise valid questions regarding the "killing contest."[19] Yamamoto would go on to write articles claiming that the Nanking massacre did not take place, and argued that the Japanese should not have to apologize for something they did not do.[20] Suzuki Akira was another journalist who denied the atrocities and felt that Chinese and Westerners "exaggerated" reports. Suzuki went on to compile a book of his articles and won literary awards for his work.[21]

The Revisionist camp began to lose credibility with the accusation that Masaaki forged some pages of the diary of Matsue Iwani, a Japanese Imperial Army officer executed for the war crimes of his soldiers.[22] Not only was that a blow to the Revisionist school, but when the diary of Japanese Lieutenant General Nakajima Kesago was printed, it held detailed records of his soldiers' daily exploits and his account "directly destroyed the scheme of the 'total denial' group's credibility such as that of Suzuki, Tanaka and many others."[23] At this point, Revisionists felt backed against a wall and in order to save their credibility, they felt forced to shift into the category of "partial" deniers.

The Revisionists separate themselves into the sub-categories of "Moderate Revisionists" and "Extreme Revisionists." Both groups agree that the Japanese Army committed some misbehavior in China, but on the issue of executing POWs, Moderates have no comment on whether it was legal, whereas the Extremes believe that the execution of POWs was legal. Both camps continue to deny the decimation of innocent civilians.[24]

As recently as 1982, the Japanese government (no doubt with influence from the Revisionist faction) revised public school textbooks. They banned the term "Nanking Massacre" and changed the term "invasion of Korea and China"[25] to "moving into Korea and China." By using a twisted syntax and tone, the government was able to downplay their factual atrocities in order to save face with their own people.

Timeline

The three previously examined schools of thought all differ on not only the number of casualties, but also the timeline in which the atrocities took place. Those who asked each faction and sub-faction for their opinions would receive a separate answer from each. Honda, of the Traditionalist camp, believed that the Japanese atrocities began when they landed at Hangchou Bay in November, not at their arrival in Nanking on December 13-17, 1937.[26] He felt it was important to include the destruction taking place between their landing in China and actually claiming victory on December 17. A fellow Traditionalist, Hiraoka Masaaki, in his work *What Did the Japanese Do In China?,* agreed that the timeline should be expanded to include what happened before December 17, but he goes so far as to say the atrocities began in August during the Shanghai Incident.[27]

Not only was there an argument as to the beginning point of the Japanese atrocities, but to the end as well. Honda argued that not all of the heinous acts by the Japanese soldiers ended when Nanking fell. In the introduction of his book, Honda says the horror continued until February of 1938.[28] From eyewitness accounts compiled throughout his work, he argued that the end-point could easily be the day the Japanese surrendered—August 15, 1945.[29]

One may ask if there is a difference in adding or subtracting a few days from the timeline, and would it really make a world of difference? It absolutely did when it came to the body count. The timeline of the Rape of Nanking may seem trivial, but it is quite important in the grand scheme of analyzing the separate schools of thought.

Playing the Numbers Game

The trend shown so far indicated that time and numbers separated the different factions. The ideology of each school depended on the timeframe and number of victims, as well as whether or not each individual school felt the Japanese Army was acting legally or illegally. It is obvious from the evidence that the Traditionalist school had the greatest number of casualties. They believed the numbers were upward of 300,000 in the few short weeks aforementioned.[30] Included in the body count were not only Chinese soldiers (during fighting), but the murders of POWs and ordinary citizens. Moderate Traditionalists used a more conservative number (although still staggering) of 150,000 to 300,000 dead.

The Centrists' numbers were much lower compared to the Traditionalists. The reason being, they did not include the murders of citizens because they denied those specific atrocities ever took place. The numbers ranged from 10,000 to 42,000 victims.[31] The Revisionist numbers, on the other hand, were incredibly and unbelievably low. They ranged anywhere from fifty victims to a maximum of 7,000.[32] Revisionists believed that atrocities against citizens were nonexistent, and the murder of POWs was legal under wartime rules, which eliminated many thousands from their count. A former Japanese Army officer, Unemoto Masami, organized a gathering of ex-officers in order to devise a number that they believed was consistent with the number of casualties witnessed. The figure they came up with was from three to six thousand killed.[33] This paltry estimate would have insulted even a Centrist.

Earlier, this paper mentioned that Honda revised his timeline to include weeks rather than the mere five days the Japanese Army was in the city of Nanking alone. Revisionist scholars were able to twist to their convenience that Honda would have needed a longer timeframe to allow for the murder of over 300,000 people, since five days was simply not long enough to complete the task. Revisionists saw this point as Honda failing to win the argument while playing the numbers game.[34] On the polar opposite side of this argument, Iris Chang argued that during the war against China, more than nineteen million people perished. She based her numbers not only on the Rape of Nanking, but also on the entire war. Included in this count were the victims of biological and chemical warfare, "medical experimentation," starvation, displacement, and disease.[35] Brooks argued that the "death toll in Nanking was higher than those of Hiroshima and Nagasaki combined" and "it is higher than the total number of civilians who died in England, France, and Belgium for the entire WWII period."[36] If correct, put into this perspective, the numbers are astounding.

The barbarity of the situation in China went far beyond the murder that was occurring on a daily basis. Rape, arson, and looting were widespread and caused just as much damage to citizens as taking the life of a member of their families. Revisionists tended to brush aside the fact that rape was occurring in extraordinary numbers, and brushed it under the carpet as nothing more than sexual "shenanigans." Eyewitnesses such as John Rabe reported rapes occurring all day, everyday, and the Japanese military set up "comfort stations" in order to curb the mass rapes that were occurring. According to author Yuki Tanaka, "Tinamura Mamoru ordered Lieutenant Colonel Cho Isamu, his junior staff officer, to carry out this task."[37] The accounts from members of the Japanese Army discredit certain Revisionist factions who deny that rapes ever occurred.

The question of "did it (the Rape of Nanking) really happen" seemed to have consensus from all factions (considering the evolution of the Revisionist school), that indeed, something took place, although the spectrum is broad on what exactly occurred. In the United States, support for Japan was failing after 1931; and by 1939, Americans were more likely to sympathize with the Chinese plight.[38] The mass media was reporting in favorite avenues such as the *New York Times*, *Washington Post*, *Reader's Digest,* and *Time Magazine*, so the average American was aware of the goings on in China; after all, "The Rape of Nanking" was a label given by the American media.[39] By the time the debates heated up again in the 1970s, it would have been difficult to say that the subject, discussed widely in the 1930s as well as again in the 1970s, was taboo.

For a journalist, an historian, a scholar, or an average person, when does the quest for the truth mutate into a war of who is "right?" Is the dividing line a fine one, or an obvious one? The schools of thought mentioned in this essay sought to explain the differing views from one extreme to the other. These factions continue to butt heads over who is correct, rather than moving forward to assure no repetition of what took place. It is far from romantic to discover a world of mass decapitation, babies bayoneted to death, innards springing forth from pregnant women, and forced rape among family members.[40] It is enough to make one sick to the stomach, although denying the events ever occurred can also induce the same effect.

Notes

1. Iris Chang, *The Rape of Nanking: The Forgotten Holocaust of World War II* (New York: Basic Books, 1997), 5.

2. Adam Gamble and Takesato Watanabe, *A Public Betrayed: An Inside Look at Japanese Media Atrocities and Their Warnings to the West* (Washington D.C.: Regnery, 2004), 265.

3. Minoru Kitamura, *The Politics of Nanjing: An Impartial Investigation*, trans. Hal Gold (Lanham: University Press of America, 2007), 5.

4. Timothy Brook, "The Tokyo Judgement and the Rape of Nanking," *The Journal of Asian Studies* 60, no. 3 (August 2001): 673.

5. Masahiro Yamamoto, *Nanking: Anatomy of an Atrocity* (Westport: Praeger Publishers, 2000), 254.

6. Ibid.

7. Ibid., 249.

8. Gamble, *A Public Betrayed*, 254.

9. Bob Wakabayashi, "The Nanking 100-Man Killing Contest Debate: War Guilt Amid Fabricated Illusions, 1971-75," *Journal of Japanese Studies* 26, no. 2 (Summer 2000): 316.

10. Ibid., 310.

11. Ibid.

12. Ibid., 309.

13. Yamamoto, *Nanking: Anatomy of an Atrocity*, 251.

14. Kitamura, *The Politics of Nanjing*, 4-5.

15. Ibid., 11.

16. Ibid., 12.

17. Yamamoto, *Nanking: Anatomy of an Atrocity*, 254.

18. FeiFei Li, Robert Sabella and David Liu, eds., *Nanking 1937: Memory and Healing* (New York: M.E. Sharpe, 2002), 6.

19. Wakabayashi, "The Nanking 100-Man Killing Contest Debate," 316.

20. Li, *Nanking 1937: Memory and Healing*, 59.

21. Ibid., 59-60.

22. Ibid., 61.

23. Ibid.

24. Yamamoto, *Nanking: Anatomy of an Atrocity*, 254.

25. Li, *Nanking 1937: Memory and Healing*, 60.

26. Yamamoto, *Nanking: Anatomy of an Atrocity*, 246.

27. Honda Katsuichi, *The Nanjing Massacre: A Japanese Journalist Confronts Japan's National Shame*, ed. Frank Gibney, trans. Karen Sandness (New York: M.E. Sharpe, 1999), 135.

28. Ibid., xxv.

29. Ibid., 135.

30. Yamamoto, *Nanking: Anatomy of an Atrocity*, 254.

31. Ibid.

32. The numbers of victims in this section were taken from Yamamoto's chart 7.1 "Rape of Nanking Controversy in Japan: Schools and Their Opinions," 254.

33. Li, *Nanking 1937*, 62.

34. Yamamoto, *Nanking: Anatomy of an Atrocity*, 246.

35. Chang, *The Rape of Nanking*, 216-217.

36. Roy L. Brooks, ed., *When Sorry Isn't Enough: The Controversy Over Apologies and Reparations forHuman Injustice* (New York: New York University Press, 1999), 104.

37. Yuki Tanaka, *Japan's Comfort Women: Sexual Slavery and Prostitution During WWII and the U.S.Occupation* (New York: Routledge, 2002), 13.

38. Takashi Yoshida, *The Making of the "Rape of Nanking" History and Memory in Japan, China, and theUnited States* (New York: Oxford University Press, 2006), 37.

39. Ibid., 38.

40. Chang, *The Rape of Nanking*, 81-99.

BIBLIOGRAPHY

Brook, Timothy. "The Tokyo Judgement and the Rape of Nanking." *The Journal of Asian Studies* 60, no. 3 (August 2001): 673-700.

Brooks, Roy L. ed., *When Sorry Isn't Enough: The Controversy over Apologies and Reparations for Human Injustice.* New York: New York University Press, 1999.

Chang, Iris. *The Rape of Nanking: The Forgotten Holocaust of World War II.* New York: Basic Books, 1997.

Gamble, Adam, and Takesato Watanabe. A *Public Betrayed: An Inside Look at Japanese Media Atrocities and Their Warnings to the West.* Washington D.C.: Regnery, 2004.

Honda, Katsuichi. *The Nanjing Massacre: A Japanese Journalist Confronts Japan's National Shame.* Edited by Frank Gibney. Translated by Karen Sandness. New York: M.E. Sharpe, 1999.

Kitamura, Minoru. *The Politics of Nanjing: An Impartial Investigation.* Translated by Hal Gold. Lanham: University Press of America, 2007.

Li, FeiFei, Robert Sabella, and David Liu, eds. *Nanking 1937: Memory and Healing.* New York: M.E. Sharpe, 2002.

Rabe, John. *The Good Man of Nanking: The Diaries of John Rabe.* Edited by Erwin Wickert. Translated by John E. Woods. New York: Alfred A. Knopf, 1998.

Tanaka, Yuki. Japan's *Comfort Women: Sexual Slavery and Prostitution during WWII and the U.S. Occupation.* New York: Routledge, 2002.

Wakabayashi, Bob. "The Nanking 100 Man Killing Contest Debate: War Guilt Amid Fabricated Illusions, 1971-75." *Journal of Japanese Studies* 26, no. 2 (Summer 2000): 307- 40.

Yamamoto, Masahiro. *Nanking: Anatomy of an Atrocity.* Westport: Praeger Publishers, 2000.

Yoshida, Takashi. *The Making of the "Rape of Nanking" History and Memory in Japan, China and the United States.* New York: Oxford University Press, 2006.

Emerging Technology and the Fourth Amendment

Kathleen Mitchell Reitmayer

Introduction

As the world moves its way well into the twenty-first century, technology is advancing at a rate never seen before in history. Most Americans have internet access, cellular phones, global positioning systems in their cars, and other technologies available at their fingertips. Technology has been the driving force in America from the beginning of the twentieth century to today.

While technology has proven to be a great time saver as well as a source of entertainment and information for the American public, technology has also created new means of both committing and tracking crime. Both the criminals and the law enforcement agents that seek the criminals can use technology. As technology advances, new ways of tracking criminals emerge. This, however, can lead to ethical and legal questions regarding the new technologies used by law enforcement.

The key use of technology by law enforcement has been to collect evidence against a criminal suspect. The rules and regulations regarding the collection of such evidence find protection under the Fourth Amendment of the United States Constitution, which reads, "[t]he right of the people to be secure in their persons, houses, papers, and effects, against unreasonable searches and seizures, shall not be violated, and no Warrants shall issue, but upon probable cause, supported by Oath or affirmation, and particularly describing the place to be searched, and the persons or things to be seized."[1]

The United States Supreme Court has been rather consistent in its findings regarding new technology as it applies to the Fourth Amendment of the United States Constitution in the latter half of the twentieth century. The Supreme Court generally refuses evidence from any new technologies used in criminal cases when obtained without a warrant as pursuant to the Fourth Amendment. The findings of the court in several cases have stated that technology used by law enforcement has been an invasion of privacy when done without a warrant, from phone tapping to the use of forward-looking infrared (FLIR).

In recent years, there has been a law created that erodes the Fourth Amendment rights that the Supreme Court has worked so hard to protect called the USA Patriot Act of 2001. This act allows for the use of some of the technology, previously found unconstitutional by the US Supreme Court, in certain cases. This is a major deviation from almost a half-century of rulings by the Supreme Court, which will open up new pathways for law enforcement to use emerging technologies in criminal cases without the suspects afforded their Fourth Amendment rights.

While the technology available for use by law enforcement advances, it is important to look at the legal and ethical aspects of the use of these new technologies. By reviewing key Supreme Court cases of the past that regarded, what was then, new, and emerging technology, and analyzing the USA Patriot Act of 2001, the legal and ethical realities of new and emerging technology will become apparent. It will then come into question whether the use of these technologies can constitute a violation of the rights of American citizens and if criminal investigations should allow the use of the technology.

Weeks v. United States

Weeks v. United States was the first key Supreme Court decision upholding the Fourth Amendment of the U. S. Constitution. While it did not have to do with technology, it laid the groundwork for further cases brought before the Supreme Court in regards to evidence collected by law enforcement by technology. The 1914 case surrounded a man by the name of Fremont Weeks. Police had arrested Weeks without a warrant and had searched his home. They accused him of being involved in a mail lottery, and they charged him with what was essentially mail fraud. They collected evidence used against him in the warrantless search of his home after his arrest.[2]

The Supreme Court found that this was a direct violation of the Fourth Amendment. Protection against an unwarranted search and the seizure of evidence from a citizen's home was the key element of the Fourth Amendment. The Supreme Court ruling clearly stated, "If letters and private documents can thus be seized and held and used in evidence against a citizen accused of an offense, the protection of the 4th Amendment, declaring his right to be secure against such searches and seizures, is of no value, and, so far as those thus placed are concerned, might as well be stricken from the Constitution."[3]

The case of *Weeks v. United States* set the precedent for all further Fourth Amendment cases. With the exception of certain circumstances, a warrant would be required for all physical searches by law enforcement. At the time of the decision, the advancement of technology did not exist that warranted any further study of technology and the Fourth Amendment. *Weeks v. US* would serve as a basis for following cases involving new technology.

Olmsted v. United States

As technology advanced into the twentieth century, the criminal element began using these technologies to advance their criminal enterprises. During the era of prohibition, the case of Roy Olmsted reached the Supreme Court of the United States. Police accused Olmsted of violating the Volstead Act and running a bootlegging operation in Washington State. The majority of the evidence collected against Mr. Olmsted was by way of wiretaps on phone lines.

Olmsted v. United States was the first Fourth Amendment case to reach the Supreme Court that questioned the legality of the use of technology in criminal investigations. The basis of the bulk of the case against Mr. Olmsted was on what they heard through the wiretaps. Law enforcement overheard detailed plans regarding the bootlegging business, in which Olmsted was allegedly involved. Olmsted argued under the precedent of *Weeks v. US*, that this constituted an illegal search and a seizure of information. However, the police had not gone on to the property to place the wiretap, instead they had connected to the telephone lines at the street level. The lack of a seizure of tangible evidence resulted in the ruling of the Supreme Court in this case.[4]

The Supreme Court found that law enforcement had not violated the Fourth Amendment in the Olmsted case. They based their ruling on the fact that no trespass had taken place to place the wires. Additionally, the Supreme Court argued, the use of telephone lines that are public domain releases the right to privacy. Unlike *Weeks v. US*, where police took sealed letters and used them as evidence, telephone lines were not sealed nor were they part of the structure and therefore were exempt from the limitations of the Fourth Amendment.[5]

This first look at technology regarding the Fourth Amendment made sense. The telephone lines were indeed not under the ownership or control of the person using them. There is no regard for privacy over public channels in terms of legality. This ruling would apply to all telephone and telegraph correspondences. This allowed law enforcement to intercept telephone call and telegraphs without a warrant and use the information collected against the accused at trial. The perspective that technology may not continue to evolve showed the Fourth Amendment could not protect the right to privacy.

Irvine v. California

The case of *Irvine v. California* was a question of the legality of placing eavesdropping devices in the home of a suspect without a warrant. Police accused Irvine of bookmaking and illegal gambling. They placed microphones and other listening devices in his residence on more than one occasion.[6] This differed from the *Olmsted v. US* case because law enforcement had entered the residence. Irvine argued that this was a violation of the Fourth Amendment on the same basis as *Weeks v. US*. The seizure of information was directly oppositional to the Fourth Amendment, and law enforcement violated Irvine's rights when they entered his home to place the listening device.

> The Supreme Court looked at the *Irvine* case from the standpoint of technological advancement and declared, That officers of the law would break and enter a home, secrete such a device, even in a bedroom, and listen to the conversation of the occupants for over a month would be almost incredible if it were not admitted. Few police measures have come to our attention that more flagrantly, deliberately, and persistently violated the fundamental principle declared by the Fourth Amendment.[7]

This, however, did not prevent them from holding up the ruling based on the fact Irvine was not arguing for any other reason than the fact that he wanted his conviction overturned.

While this did nothing to change the rule of law in regards to emerging technologies, the Supreme Court's ruling surely looked down upon the means of collecting evidence. It was, as stated, a violation of the Fourth Amendment rights of the accused. Further dealing with technology used by law enforcement would refer back to the *Irvine* case.

Silverman v. United States

The case of *Silverman v. United States* revolved around an illegal gambling house in Washington, DC. Law enforcement, with the permission of the neighbors in an adjoining row house, had placed a microphone under the baseboards to reach the ventilation system of the suspect residence in order to gain information about suspected gambling operations taking place.[8] Much like the *Irvine v. CA* case a few years earlier, it argued that law enforcement had trespassed into the residence without a warrant and due to this had directly violated the Fourth Amendment of the United States Constitution. This was in accordance with the *Olmsted v. US* decision a violation. Where *Olmsted v. US* had stated the wiretapping at street level was not a violation due to the fact law enforcement had not entered the residence, in this case since they had entered the residence, it was a violation.

The Supreme Court overturned the decision based on *Olmstead v. US*. The act of trespassing by law enforcement was enough to make the eavesdropping unconstitutional under the Fourth Amendment. Any further attempt at eavesdropping by law enforcement would require a warrant to be admissible in criminal court. This directly overruled the *Irvine v. California* case.

Katz v. United States

The case of Charles Katz was a major turning point in the legal aspects of technology. Police accused Katz of bookmaking and collected the evidence against him through a wiretap on a phone booth he frequented to make wagers. *Katz v. United States* was almost identical to the *Olmsted v. United States* case. The argument was the same that there was an implied privacy when one was using a telephone. More importantly, in the *Katz* case, the use of a public telephone, which he argued, was a "constitutionally protected area."[9]

While the members of law enforcement had assumed they had the right to wiretap the phone under the protection of the *Olmsted* ruling, the Supreme Court questioned the rationality of not getting a warrant, which would have been attainable in the case. The Supreme Court argued that individual police officers should not make the decision as to who they are to wiretap or not. The Supreme Court questioned the ruling in *Olmsted v. US* stating that they had made the decision without the view toward new technology.

The Supreme Court ruled that wiretapping anywhere was a direct violation of the Fourth Amendment based partially on the *Silverman v. US* ruling. They decided that seizure was to include non-tangible information such as that gained from wiretapping or eavesdropping pursuant to the *Silverman v. US* decision. The Supreme Court ruling extended the Fourth Amendment to protect the privacy of the individual citizen, regardless of location without a search warrant.

This is a major roadblock in the use of new and emerging technology by law enforcement. The *Katz v. US* ruling declared any attempts at collecting information by the means of technology without a warrant illegal. This protected the American people from technological invasions of privacy that are in line with the Fourth Amendment of the United States Constitution.

Kyllo v. United States

The *Kyllo v. United States* case regarded a marijuana grower in Oregon. Law enforcement had used FLIR cameras to survey Kyllo's home for heat signatures consistent with lights used to cultivate marijuana plants indoors. They used the heat signatures found in the surveillance to get a warrant to search the residence where they found marijuana plants.[10] Lawyers argued *Kyllo v. US* under the precedence of *Katz v. US* stating that it was an invasion of the privacy of the resident to use this new technology to attain a search warrant. By using the FLIR technology, law enforcement had garnered information not attainable without looking into the residence.

The Supreme Court ruled in the favor of Kyllo with an eye toward future technology. With technological advances from aerial surveillance to through the wall sound recording, it was the opinion of the Supreme Court that such uses of technology were intrusive as per the *Katz v. United States* ruling. The Fourth Amendment of the United States Constitution must protect the privacy of the individual when it comes to law enforcement and technology.

USA Patriot Act of 2001

While the United States Supreme Court has progressively tightened the restriction on law enforcement and the use of new and emergent technology, the Patriot Act served to unravel the laws built over the past century in the United States regarding the Fourth Amendment of the United States Constitution. Title II of the Patriot Act now allowed the United States government to conduct wiretaps without a warrant in direct opposition of *Katz v. United States*. Not only does it allow law enforcement to gather information by these means without a warrant; they are required to report them. This is a violation of the Fourth Amendment. Although closely held that this is only for use in the case of international terrorism, it provides for a loophole through which authorities could possibly put non-terrorists under surveillance.[11] It is impossible to believe that when this Act comes before the Supreme Court of the United States, they will uphold it given the long-standing and progressive stance the Supreme Court has taken on the Fourth Amendment.

Emerging Technology

People create new technologies to enhance the work of law enforcement against organized crime every day. As technology advances, so does the means by which criminals can conduct business. From computers and internet-based crimes to the use of cellular phones to conduct everyday business, the criminal world is now more technologically advanced. The Federal Bureau of Investigation has moved right along with the new technology to catch organized criminals. Since 1999, the FBI has had Regional Computer Forensics Laboratory sites across the United States.[12] This has allowed the FBI to do appropriate computer searches under the Fourth Amendment. Additionally, the FBI continues to conduct wiretaps and other visual and digital surveillance with a commitment to protecting the Fourth Amendment rights of individuals.[13]

While the public knows many of the technological capabilities of law enforcement, some remain unknown for the protection of the information. What the public knows are new and interesting uses of technology. One example would be cellular phone triangulation, which can pinpoint the location where someone last used a cellular phone. This could place a suspect and the scene of a crime for use against organized crime. Getting this information, according to the Fourth Amendment, would include getting a warrant for the phone records. Additionally, many cars now have built in global positioning systems which could provide useful data to law enforcement regarding where and when suspects were at a location.

Conclusion

Over the past century, technology has grown exponentially. Both organized crime and law enforcement have been able to keep up with the pace of technology in America. As each new technology comes into place, there comes a question of what is legal and constitutional to listen to or see on the part of law enforcement. This question of technology and the Fourth Amendment has come before the Supreme Court of the United States on several occasions. The Supreme Court has broadened the spectrum of the Fourth Amendment on several occasions to protect the citizens of the United States of America.

Each general type of emerging technology has come to question before the Supreme Court. From the telephone in *Olmsted v. US* and *Katz v. US*, microphones in *Silverman v. US*, and FLIR usage in *Kyllo v. US*, the United States has questioned evidence obtained via new technology. As each new technology makes its way onto the scene, the Supreme Court has answered the question of whether law enforcement is over-stepping its bounds with the usage with a resounding "yes." This sets the precedent for the use of new technology. One would be remiss not say that, in accordance with the Fourth Amendment, any form of new technology should not be used without an appropriate warrant to protect the rights of the suspects. The founding fathers of the United States wanted it to be this way.

Technology is a great advantage to law enforcement. Having information that definitely declares a suspect guilty beyond a reasonable doubt is much easier when the bulk of the information is coming from irrefutable evidence such as wiretaps of crime planning, being able to place a suspect at a specific location from cellular phone records, or having written evidence that has come from a computer. This, however, must balance with respect toward the suspect's Fourth Amendment rights. If a warrant is not in place, police should not, and cannot use the evidence against the suspect in court. The Fourth Amendment will always trump new technology and that is how it should be in America.

Notes

1. *U.S. Constitution*, amend. 4.

2. *Weeks v. United States*, 232 U.S. 383 (1914).

3. Ibid.

4. *Olmsted v. United States*, 277 U.S. 438 (1928).

5. Ibid.

6. *Irvine v. California*, 347 U.S. 128 (1954).

7. Ibid.

8. *Silverman v. United States*, 365 U.S. 505 (1961).

9. *Katz v. United States*, 389 U.S. 347 (1967).

10. *Kyllo v. United States*, 533 U.S. 27 (2001).

11. USA Patriot Act (2001).

12. "Introduction to RCFLs Fact Sheet," Introduction to RCFLs Fact Sheet, www.rcfl.gov/downloads/documents/intro_to_RCFLs.pdf (accessed October 10, 2011).

13. "FBI Capabilities," FBI Homepage, http://www.fbi.gov/about-us/otd/capabilities (accessed October 10, 2011).

BIBLIOGRAPHY

"FBI Capabilities." *FBI Homepage.* http://www.fbi.gov/about-us/otd/capabilities
(accessed October 10, 2011).

"Introduction to RCFLs Fact Sheet." Introduction to RCFLs Fact Sheet.
www.rcfl.gov/downloads/documents/intro_to_RCFLs.pdf. (accessed
October 10, 2011).

Irvine v. California, 347 U.S. 128 (1954).

Katz v. United States, 389 U.S. 347 (1967).

Kyllo v. United States, 533 U.S. 27 (2001).

Olmsted v. United States, 277 U.S. 438 (1928).

Silverman v. United States, 365 U.S. 505 (1961).

U.S. Constitution, amend. 4.

USA Patriot Act (2001).

Weeks v. United States, 232 U.S. 383 (1914).

Cultural History and the World of Johan Huizinga

Anne Midgley

By his own admission and intention, Huizinga was a cultural historian, a man who deliberately brought back into historical study material appropriated by the art historian, the historian of literature, the folklorist, the sociologist; a man who dealt with "culture," both present and past, in his works; a man whose life and works pose cultural problems of their own.

—R. L. Colie

Poignant and perceptive, Johan Huizinga (1872-1945) displayed an eerie foresight when he wrote the opening and closing lines of the foreword to *Homo Ludens*, his landmark theoretical study of the history of play in June 1938. "A HAPPIER age than ours once made bold to call our species by the name of *Homo Sapiens* . . . I had to write now, or not at all. And I wanted to write."[1] Perhaps he guessed that far worse days lay ahead and that he would not survive the hell created in Europe by Hitler. However prescient his words may have been, Huizinga's influence remains very much with the world today and is seen in areas ranging from medieval and cultural history to the design of computer games.[2]

Heir to the cultural history historiography tradition of Herodotus, Johan Huizinga is an ideal representative of one of the two forms of cultural history that developed in northern Europe during the latter part of the nineteenth century. According to Bentley's classification of nineteenth century cultural history in "Culture and Kultur," Huizinga belongs to the camp that sought to comprehend the past "from the history of art and literature as keys to understanding social perception and the limits of a period's sense of itself."[3] Huizinga follows in the footsteps of the great Swiss historian, Jacob Burckhardt, whose work *The Civilization of the Renaissance in Italy* provides "cross-sections dealing with aspects of the Renaissance environment . . . in a new literature concerned with 'the daily course of human life.'"[4] Huizinga's own landmark work of cultural history, *Herfsttij der Middeleeuwen: Studie over levens- en gedachtenvormen der veertiende en vijftiende eeuw in Frankrijk en de Nederlanden,* originally written in

109

Dutch, has since been published in sixteen languages. Two English translations exist, *The Waning of the Middle Ages: A Study of the Forms of Life, Thought and Art in France and the Netherlands in the XIVth and XVth Centuries,* translated by Fritz Hopman and published in 1924, and the more recent *The Autumn of the Middle Ages,* translated by Rodney J. Payton and Ulrich Mammitzsch, and published in 1996.[5]

This research paper will attempt to trace the historiographical influences that shaped Huizinga's work, to place his writing in the broader tradition of cultural history, and to link Huizinga's work to the New Cultural History movement of the late twentieth century.[6]

Ernst Breisach claims Burckhardt was "the most influential representative of modern cultural history" with Huizinga following in his footsteps and adding substantially to that great "tradition."[7] Peter Burke places both Burckhardt and Huizinga in the category of "classic" cultural historians. Burke defines the period of classic cultural history as that running from the beginning of the nineteenth century to the mid-point of the twentieth century. Burckhardt, the elder of these two titans of cultural history and known as its "founder," used art as one of the key elements upon which he built his masterpiece, *The Civilization of the Renaissance in Italy,* as did Huizinga later in *Autumn.* Both men were "amateur artists as well as art lovers and they began their famous books in order to understand certain works by placing them in their historical context."[8] Burckhardt strove to lay bare the essence of the age of the Italian Renaissance, beginning his study with the brutal, strife-filled world of the tyrants and condottieri of the Italian city-states, describing the murder, betrayal, lust, and mayhem caused by the rapid rise and speedier fall of these despots. Like his successor, Huizinga, Burckhardt's prose sweeps across the daily life of both the exalted and the lowly, touching on morality, religion, literature, art, festivals and carnivals, witches and poets. Certain of Burckhardt's points of emphasis reappear in Huizinga's *Autumn* in an eerily similar fashion. Take, for example, this instance of religious fervor provided by Burckhardt, "The concluding sermon is a general benediction . . . throngs of hearers accompany the preacher to the next city, and there listen for a second time to the whole course of sermons"[9] compared to Huizinga's description of the power that itinerant preachers held over the people "When he informed his audience after his tenth sermon that it would have to be his last . . . a large number . . . leave the city...and spend the night out in the fields in order to secure good places [to listen again to his sermon]."[10]

Henri Pirenne, the Belgian economic and social historian, also played an influential role in shaping Huizinga's view of the Burgundian late medieval period. Pirenne saw the origins of Belgium "in the Middle Ages when, long before political unification, a cultural and social unity emerged which justified a 'history of a civilisation' such as the *Histoire de Belgique*."[11] Their similar interests in the impact of the Dukes of Burgundy on the development of the Low Countries led to a long-term, often strained, professional relationship, but Huizinga saw Pirenne as a role model until the end of his life.[12]

Burckhardt's writings undoubtedly played a tremendous role in the development of Huizinga as an historian; "Huizinga was in a real sense Burckhardt's first great pupil."[13] Huizinga refers to his predecessor a number of times in *Autumn*. In these references, it is clear that Burckhardt needs no introduction to Huizinga's intended audience; it is presumed that the reader knows Burckhardt and his work. While admiring Burckhardt, Huizinga also gently criticizes his predecessor's position on the Middle Ages, as Huizinga strives to support his own thesis that the late medieval period was not so different a period from Burckhardt's Renaissance. Huizinga defends the emphasis of Burgundians on "personal honor and fame . . . [as a] characteristic quality of Renaissance man" and states "Burckhardt has judged the distance between medieval and Renaissance times and between western Europe and Italy to be too great."[14] Huizinga specifically cites Burckhardt in a number of instances within *Autumn*, including pages 15, 43, 73-74, 173-174 and indirectly refers to Burckhardt's theories and Huizinga's counter-point position in many additional places, including pages 39-41 and 43. Interestingly, Huizinga also disagrees with Burckhardt over the latter's views expressed about the "contest" as a key element in life. Burckhardt, whose early writing focused on classical Greece, confined agonistic man to the ancient Greeks, while Huizinga saw the "contest" as a form of "play," and "play" as older than civilization itself and found in all aspects of the life of man.[15]

Cultural history did not begin with Burckhardt. Cultural history's roots can be traced back to Herodotus, with his broad-ranging inquiry and focus on peoples beyond the Greek and the great. Burke asserts that cultural history was found in Germany in the eighteenth century, while Bentley claims it essentially began with the German journal *Zeitschrift für deutsche Kulturgeschichte* in 1856. Burke and Bentley, however, both see Burckhardt as a monumental cultural historian, though one whose influence did not at once make its mark. Huizinga carried Burckhardt's standard, and similar to his predecessor, Huizinga's influence was primarily felt by later cultural historians, much more so than those of his own day. In a sense, both Burckhardt and Huizinga foreshadowed the New Cultural History movement, as each retreated to it as a "spiritual refuge" in reaction to social upheavals: Burckhardt reacting to the revolutions in Europe during 1848, Huizinga to the immense catastrophe of the Great War.[16]

Huizinga himself provided a succinct description of cultural history through his essay "The Task of the Cultural Historian." He states that "Cultural history is distinct from political and economic history in that it is worthy of the name only to the extent that it concentrates on deeper, general themes. . . . Only when the scholar turns to determining the patterns of life, art, and thought taken all together can there actually be a question of cultural history."[17]

Before tracing the impacts that Huizinga has had on later generations of historians, it is worthwhile to explore the forces that shaped his world view and historical thought. Professor Huizinga was himself the son of a university professor. He attended the University of Groningen, studied literature, history, and comparative philology, and attained his doctoral degree in 1897, having completed his dissertation on a Sanskrit drama. "Philology taught him a very important lesson: that the history of language . . . was not the record of stages of individual words, but one record, in vocabulary and syntax, of social life."[18] As a young man, Huizinga experienced a number of events which shaped his later fascination with the art of the Van Eycks and the late medieval period, among them, his "memory of the ambitious pageant staged at Groningen commemorating the entry of Edzard, count of East Friesland into Groningen in 1506," great exhibits of early "Netherlandish" works of art, and his interest in the idea of a Northern Renaissance.[19] Huizinga traveled abroad and knew the great Italian Renaissance works of art firsthand. He spent several years reading famous court chroniclers, including Chastellain, Monstrelet, and Froissart, as well as the poet Deschamps, and he relied extensively on their writings to interpret the late medieval "spirit of the age."[20] His early focus on Indian literature and culture gave way to a greater emphasis on the history of the Low Countries and a fascination with America, which included publishing a study on American culture prior to the publication of his great *Autumn* in 1919. In 1905, he "was called to the chair of Netherlands history at the University of Groningen" and later went to the University of Leiden, where he remained until the university "closed its doors in protest against the dismissal of its Jewish professors" following the German occupation of 1940.[21] He resigned from Leiden in 1942, was arrested for insubordination by the Germans, sent to a detention camp and later released. Huizinga wrote his autobiography during the war years and died in "the ravaging Dutch winter of 1944-45 when no food could be found."[22]

Beyond Burckhardt and Pirenne, a remarkable list of historians, sociologists, philosophers, poets and literary critics, including Karl Lamprecht, Alexis de Tocqueville, Karl Mannheim, Max Weber, Willem Kloos, Emile Mâle, and Karl Voll influenced Huizinga.[23] Later in his life, Huizinga became friends with Marc Bloch, and Bloch and his partner Lucien Febvre invited him to contribute to the *Annales*, in response to Huizinga's reversing his life-long aversion to politics and taking a stand against an anti-Semitic historian, Johannes von Leers by prohibiting von Leers access to the University of Leiden.[24]

Huizinga's celebrated works include the previously mentioned *The Autumn of the Middle Ages* and *Homo Ludens*, as well as *Erasmus* and *Dutch Culture in the Seventeenth Century*. Other works include *Man and Mass in America, American Living and Thinking,* "The Task of Cultural History," *In the Shadow of Tomorrow: A Diagnosis of the Spiritual Ills of Our Time, The World in Ruins: A Consideration of the Chances of Restoring Our Civilization,* and, at his wife's request, "My Way to History."[25] From their titles alone, it is easy to place *In the Shadow of Tomorrow* and *The World in Ruins* as works flowing from the gathering storm and its aftermath in Europe following the rise of the National Socialist Party in Germany. Huizinga, who by inclination, training, and experience was a broad-based intellectual, responded to the growing darkness of his own times by becoming a cultural critic, a departure from his earlier persona of cultural historian. It is through this transition, coupled with his outstanding international reputation as a cultural historian, that he made his legacy.[26]

Huizinga's most well-known work, *Autumn,* argued that the culture of the fourteenth and fifteenth centuries in France and the Netherlands was not "announcing the Renaissance, but [were] as the end of the Middle Ages, as the age of medieval thought in its last phase of life, as a tree with overripe fruits, fully unfolded and developed."[27] He defines much that has been attributed to the Renaissance to in fact be characteristic of the medieval period. Huizinga's examples range from an analysis of the work of Jan van Eyck, concluding that van

Eyck's art, while often regarded as "announcing the arrival of the Renaissance, should rather be regarded as the complete unfolding of the medieval spirit"[28] to a discussion of the rise of Humanism, claiming that Petrarch, the "first modern man of letters" was rather a scholar still firmly based in the "medieval spirit."[29] Huizinga's prose immerses the reader in the fourteenth and fifteenth centuries of northern Europe. He freely draws upon the court chroniclers, most frequently Jean Froissart, Olivier de la Marche, Georges Chastellain, and Enguerrand de Monstrelet. He paints a world vastly different than that of the early twentieth century with his opening "When the world was half a thousand years younger all events had much sharper outlines . . . all things in life had about them something glitteringly and cruelly public."[30] Huizinga is at his strongest as he builds sights, sounds, smells, color, and emotion into the portrait he paints of the age. The reader is swept away.

Figure 1. *The Annunciation.* Jan van Eyck. Oil on canvas transferred from panel. 1434-1436. National Gallery of Art.

Huizinga, who strongly opposed the practices of positivist historians, cautions historians in several places within *Autumn* against relying on official records alone to construct the past, as in doing so the historian will fail to appreciate "the unrestrained extravagance and inflammability of the medieval heart" as "the documents tell us little about the difference in tone that separates us from those times."[31] Huizinga admits that the official documents contain the most reliable information for the history of the period, though they do little to portray the tenor of the times.[32] Huizinga clearly illustrates the value that cultural history provides to the understanding of an age in this amusing passage:

> But the history of culture has just as much to do with dreams of beauty and the illusions of a noble life as with population figures and statistics. A more recent scholar, having studied today's society in terms of the growth of banks and traffic, of political and military conflicts, would be able to state at the end of his studies: "I have noticed very little about music, which obviously had little meaning for this culture.[33]

Responses to *Autumn* and Huizinga's other works have varied greatly from the time of their publication to the present day. *Autumn* did not please adherents of the positivist view. Critics, including R. L. Colie, Pieter Geyl, Th. J. G. Locher, and Jan Romein felt that *Autumn* lacked political history. Of *Autumn*, Locher stated, "Oh, yes, it is wonderful, but of course, it isn't history."[34] *Autumn* did have a significant influence on several younger intellectuals of his day, including Ernst Kantorowicz, "whose own intellectual and artistic development . . . oddly parallels that of Huizinga" and Norbert Elias.[35] Elias, a disciple of Max Weber, "produced . . . *The Civilizing Process* (1939), which is essentially a cultural history."[36] Burke claims that Elias built upon Huizinga's constructs and methods in his study of table manners in Western Europe.[37] *Autumn* reflects Huizinga's prejudices and biases, frequently in a manner that would be seen as unfitting for a twenty-first century historian. *Autumn* contains frequent passages that underscore its author's strong Protestant background; Huizinga was the "descendant of a long line of Mennonite pastors."[38] Examples of Huizinga's prose reflecting his Protestant prejudice of Catholic countries and cultures include "In a primitive culture—I have for example, the Irish in mind," to "In our own time the same differences in temperament separates the Latin peoples from their northern neighbors; those in the south accept contradictions more readily."[39]

Surprisingly, while the interests of Huizinga and those of the *Annales* founders, Bloch and Febvre, were quite similar, their interaction appears to have been fairly limited and not fruitful to the work of either Huizinga or the *Annales* founders.[40]

Huizinga's star ascended in the mid-1960s "by the venerations expressed by Karl Joachim Weintraub" a University of Chicago professor of cultural history, and teacher of a Western Civilization course so popular with students that they camped out in the university quad to ensure themselves of a place in his class.[41] With the rediscovery of the power of cultural history in the latter part of the twentieth century, Huizinga's star reached its apogee. The long list of luminaries claiming Huizinga as an innovator of cultural history includes Gerd Althoff, Georges Duby, Jacques Le Goff, and Peter Burke.[42]

Adherents of the New Cultural History (NCH) movement and those who subscribed to the "anthropological turn" found new insights from the study of symbolism, which had been a key focus within Huizinga's *Autumn*. New emphasis arose, however, including the cultural history of women, which is only dimly felt in Huizinga's work, but clearly articulated in NCH works, such as those of Caroline Bynum's *Holy Feast and Holy Fast* (1987).[43]

Other more recent currents in cultural history echo Huizinga in other ways as well. The focus on folklore found in the history of popular culture had glimpses of what was to be in *Autumn*. What Burke referred to as the "visual turn" has extremely strong precedents in Huizinga's *Autumn*, with Huizinga's focus on the art of van Eycks as depicting a rich view into the full life of the Burgundians.[44] Huizinga's *Autumn* uses an emphasis on the quality and texture of sound to provide historical insight; "One sound rose ceaselessly above the noises of busy life and lifted all things unto a sphere of order and serenity: the sound of bells. The bells were in daily life like good spirits . . . they were known by their names . . . everyone knew the difference in meaning of the various ways of ringing."[45] This emphasis, too, has found more recent disciples in those that explore the "cultural history of perception" such as historian Simon Schama, as he describes sights, smells, and sounds in *Rembrandt's Eyes* (1999).[46]

More so than his emphasis on art, folklore, perception through physical senses or symbolism, though, Huizinga returns time and again throughout *Autumn* to a need to understand the Burgundian late Middle Ages "spirit of the age" through a focus on emotions. His sources, from the chroniclers, to the poets, to the art of the age are all used to better understand "The Passionate Intensity of Life" best displayed through his first chapter of *Autumn* of the same name. Treating emotions in history is not as common as some, particularly Barbara H. Rosenwein, might hope. Rosenwein's fascinating essay "Worrying about Emotions in History," traces the historiography of emotions in history. Rosenwein references both Huizinga and Febvre as early proponents of study of history through a focus on emotions. Surprisingly, Rosenwein believes that Febvre's call for a focus on the study of emotions was in fact, a criticism of Huizinga's *Autumn*, as Febvre objected that Huizinga did not put enough stress on the violent, passionate nature of emotions in life. However, the focus on emotions in history has since been subject to much greater emphasis and study. Norbert Elias focused on the cultural history of emotions, using Huizinga's work as his stepping stone. Carol and Peter Stearns "have published a manifesto for historical 'emotionology,'" while William Reddy, in *The Navigation of Feeling* (2001), draws on both anthropology and psychology to examine emotions in history.[47]

Jay Winter speaks of the "affective turn" in recent cultural history, claiming that in recent years "scholars have been more open to developing historical interpretations with the benefit of insights derived from literary studies, anthropology, psychology, and the history of art and music."[48] How very Huizinga-esque!

Not only did Johan Huizinga benefit from the influences of some of the great historiographical masters of the late nineteenth and early twentieth century, but his cultural history blended key influences from anthropology, art history, linguistics, philosophy, psychology, and sociology. The historiographical influences that shaped Huizinga's work continue to be felt in the broader tradition of cultural history, and clearly link Huizinga's work to the New Cultural History movement of the late twentieth century and today. In rediscovering the merits of cultural history in the 1970s, historians were reacting "against earlier approaches to the past which left out something at once elusive and important."[49] As Huizinga clearly showed in *Autumn*, there is a vast divide between the present of his day and today to the late medieval period. To understand that period better, one must gain an emotional sense of the time, to understand, for instance, as Huizinga describes, that the "modern city hardly knows pure darkness or true silence anymore, nor does it know the effect of a single small light or that lonely distant shout."[50] It is this power to evoke the past that Huizinga mastered so well, and that cultural historians of today seek to provide.

Notes

1. Johan Huizinga, *Homo Ludens: A Study of the Play-Element in Culture* (1950; repr., Boston: The Beacon Press, 1955), xvi-xvii. Huizinga's quote "A HAPPIER age than ours once made bold to call our species by the name of *Homo Sapiens* . . . I had to write now, or not at all" reflected the dark days in Europe of 1938 and his observation that Homo Sapiens—"wise man"—no longer seemed to be an appropriate name for the modern human species.

2. Robert Anchor, "History and Play: Johan Huizinga and His Critics," *History and Theory* 17, no. 1 (February 1978): 63, http://www.jstor.org/stable/2504901 (Accessed May 11, 2011); COMP 590: *Serious Games*, The University of North Carolina at Chapel Hill, http://www.unc.edu/search/index.htm?cx=014532668884084418890%3Ajyc_iub1byy&cof=FORID%3A10&ie=UTF-8&q=Huizinga#1019 (Accessed June 18, 2011).

3. Michael Bentley, *Modern Historiography: An Introduction (*1999; repr., New York: Routledge, 2010), 53.

4. Ibid., 55.

5. WorldCat Identities, "Most widely held works by Johan Huizinga," http://www.worldcat.org/identities/lccn-n50-34372 (accessed May 3, 2011); Johan Huizinga, *The Waning of the Middle Ages: A Study of the Forms of Life, Thought and Art in France and The Netherlands in the XIVth and XVth Centuries,* trans. F. Hopman (1924; repr., New York: St. Martin's Press, 1984); Johan Huizinga, *The Autumn of the Middle Ages,* trans. Rodney J. Payton and Ulrich Mammitzsch (Chicago: The University of Chicago Press, 1996).

6. Ernst Breisach, *Historiography: Ancient, Medieval, and Modern* 3rd ed. (Chicago: The University of Chicago Press, 1983), 425.

7. Ibid.

8. Peter Burke, *What is Cultural History?* 2nd ed. (2008; repr., Malden, MA: Polity, 2010), 7; Martina Sitt, "Jacob Burckhardt as Architect of a New Art History," *Journal of the Warburg and Courtauld Institutes* 57, (1994): 227-242, www.jstor.org/stable/751471 (Accessed June 24, 2011).

9. Jacob Burckhardt, *The Civilization of the Renaissance in Italy,* trans. S. G. C. Middlemore (London: MacMillan and Co., 1904), 471.

10. Huizinga, *Autumn*, 5.

11. Jo Tollebeek, "At the crossroads of nationalism: Huizinga, Pirenne and the Low Countries in Europe," *European Review of History – Revue européenne d'histoire* 17, no. 2 (April 2010): 188.

12. Ibid., 187-215.

13. Colie, "Huizinga," 611.

14. Huizinga, *Autumn*, 74.

15. Huizinga, *Homo Ludens*, 71-74.

16. Breisach, *Historiography*, 18, 304; Burke, *Cultural History*, 6; Bentley, *Historiography*, 53; Huizinga, *Homo Ludens*, 71; Peter Burke, "Huizinga, Prophet of 'Blood and Roses'" *History Today* (November 1986): 25.

17. Anchor, "History and Play," 65.

18. Colie, "Huizinga," 611-12.

19. Edward Peters and Walter P. Simons, "The New Huizinga and the Old Middle Ages," *Speculum* 74 (1999): 596-597, http://www.jstor.org/stable/2886762 (Accessed May 3, 2011).

20. Peters and Simons, "The New Huizinga,"596-597; Bentley, *Historiography*, 61; Burke, "Huizinga," 24.

21. Peters and Simons, "The New Huizinga," 597; Colie, "Huizinga," 610.

22. Bentley, *Historiography*, 61.

23. Edward Peters and Walter P. Simons, "The New Huizinga," 597, 600, 602; Colie, "Huizinga," 608, 620.

24. Colie, "Huizinga," 619; Tollebeek, "At the crossroads of nationalism," 199.

25. Colie, "Huizinga," 609, 611, 613; H. L. Wesseling, "From cultural historian to cultural critic: Johan Huizinga and the spirit of the 1930s," *European Review*, 10, no. 4 (2002): 485 – 499, http://search.proquest.com.ezproxy1.apus.edu/docview/217354157?accountid=8289 (Accessed July 2, 2011).

26. Colie, "Huizinga," 613; Wesseling, "From cultural historian to cultural critic," 485.

27. Huizinga, *Autumn*, xix.

28. Ibid., 319.

29. Francis Petrarch, "Letter to Cicero," *Hanover Historical Texts Project,* (1995-96), http://history.hanover.edu/courses/excerpts/111pet2.html (accessed June 1, 2011); Huizinga, *Autumn*, 1.

30. Huizinga, *Autumn*, 1.

31. Ibid., 8-15; Edward Peters and Walter P. Simons, "The New Huizinga," 601.

32. Huizinga, *Autumn*, 15.

33. Huizinga, *Autumn*, 103.

34. Colie, "Huizinga," 614.

35. Edward Peters and Walter P. Simons, "The New Huizinga," 614.

36. Burke, *Cultural History,* 10.

37. Ibid., 10-11.

37. Edward Peters and Walter P. Simons, "The New Huizinga," 596.

39. Huizinga, *Autumn*, 56, 203.

40. Wesseling, "From cultural historian to cultural critic," 490.

41. Edward Peters and Walter P. Simons, "The New Huizinga," 601; Karl Joachim Weintraub, The University of Chicago News Office, March 24, 2004, http://www-news.uchicago.edu/releases/04/040326.weintraub.shtml (Accessed July 2, 2011).

42. Edward Peters and Walter P. Simons, "The New Huizinga," 616-617.

43. Breisach, *Historiography,* 425; Burke, *Cultural History,* 41, 49-50.

44. Peter Burke, "History and Folklore: A Historiographical Survey," *Folklore,* 115, no. 2 (August 2004): 135, http://search.proquest.com.ezproxy2.apus.edu/docview/202751693?accountid=8289 (Accessed July 2, 2011): Peter Burke, "Picturing history," *History Today,* 51, no. 4 (April 2001): 22-23, http://search.proquest.com.ezproxy2.apus.edu/docview/202815330?accountid=8289 (Accessed July 2, 2011).

45. Huizinga, *Waning*, 2.

46. Burke, *Cultural History*, 112.

47. Huizinga, *Autumn*, 1-29; Barbara J. Rosenwein, "Worrying about Emotions in History," *The American Historical Review,* 107, no. 3 (June 2002): 823, 821-845, http://www.jstor.org/stable/10.1086/532498 (Accessed May 28, 2011); Burke, *Cultural History,* 110-111.

48. Jay Winter, Reviewed work(s): *On the Battlefield of Memory: The First World War and American Remembrance, 1919-1941* by Steven Trout and *The "Good War" in American Memory* by John Bodnar, *The American Historical Review*, 116, no. 3 (June 2011): 755-758, http://www.jstor.org/stable/10.1086/ahr.116.3.755 (Accessed July 2, 2011).

49. Burke, *Cultural History*, 1.

50. Huizinga, *Autumn*, 2.

BIBLIOGRAPHY

Anchor, Robert. "History and Play: Johan Huizinga and His Critics." *History and Theory* 17, no. 1 (February 1978): 63-93. http://www.jstor.org/ stable/2504901 (Accessed May 11, 2011).

Bentley, Michael. *Modern Historiography: An Introduction.* 1999. Reprint, New York: Routledge, 2010.

Breisach, Ernst A. *Historiography: Classic, Medieval, and Modern*, 3rd ed. Chicago: University of Chicago Press, 2007.

Burckhardt, Jacob. *The Civilization of the Renaissance in Italy.* Translated by S. G. C. Middlemore. London: MacMillan and Co., 1904.

Burke, Peter. "History and Folklore: A Historiographical Survey." *Folklore,* 115, no. 2 (August 2004): 133-139. http:// search.proquest.com.ezproxy2.apus.edu/docview/202751693? accountid=8289 (Accessed July 2, 2011).

_____. "Huizinga, Prophet of 'Blood and Roses.'" *History Today,* (November, 1986): 23-28.

_____. "Picturing history." *History Today,* 51, no. 4 (April 2001): 22-23. http:// search.proquest.com.ezproxy2.apus.edu/docview/202815330? accountid=8289 (Accessed July 2, 2011).

_____. *What is Cultural History?* 2nd ed. 2008. Reprint, Malden, MA: Polity, 2010.

Colie, R. L. "Johan Huizinga and the Task of Cultural History." *The American Historical Review* LXIX, no. 3 (April 1964): 607-630. http:// www.jstor.org/stable/1845780 (Accessed May 15, 2011).

COMP 590: *Serious Games*. The University of North Carolina at Chapel Hill. http://www.unc.edu/search/index.htm?cx=014532668884084418890% 3Ajyc_iub1byy&cof=FORID%3A10&ie=UTF-8&q=Huizinga#1019 (Accessed June 18, 2011).

Huizinga, Johan. *Homo Ludens: A Study of the Play-Element in Culture.* 1950. Reprint, Boston: The Beacon Press, 1955.

_____. *The Autumn of the Middle Ages.* Translated by Rodney J. Payton and

Ulrich Mammitzsch. Chicago: The University of Chicago Press, 1996.

_____. *The Waning of the Middle Ages: A Study of the Forms of Life, Thought and Art in France and The Netherlands in the XIVth and XVth Centuries.* Translated by F. Hopman. 1924. Reprint, New York: St. Martin's Press, 1984.

Rosenwein, Barbara H. "Worrying about Emotions in History." *The American Historical Review* 107, no. 3 (June 2002): 821-845. http://www.jstor.org/ stable/10.1086/532498 (Accessed May 28, 2011).

Sitt, Martina. "Jacob Burckhardt as Architect of a New Art History." *Journal of the Warburg and Courtauld Institutes* 57, (1994), 227-242. www.jstor.org/ stable/751471 (Accessed June 24, 2011).

Tollebeek, Jo. "At the crossroads of nationalism: Huizinga, Pirenne and the Low Countries in Europe." *European Review of History – Revue européenne d'histoire* 17, no. 2 (April 2010): 187-215.

Wesseling, H. L., "From cultural historian to cultural critic: Johan Huizinga and the spirit of the 1930s." *European Review*, 10, no. 4 (2002): 185 – 499. http:// search.proquest.com.ezproxy1.apus.edu/docview/217354157? accountid=8289 (Accessed July 2, 2011).

Winter, Jay. Reviewed work(s): *On the Battlefield of Memory: The First World War and American Remembrance, 1919-1941* by Steven Trout and *The "Good War" in American Memory* by John Bodnar, *The American Historical Review*, 116, no. 3 (June 2011): 755-758. http://www.jstor.org/ stable/10.1086/ahr.116.3.755 (Accessed July 2, 2011).

WorldCat Identities. "Most widely held works by Johan Huizinga." http:// www.worldcat.org/identities/lccn-n50-34372 (accessed May 3, 2011).

John Ferling. *Independence: The Struggle to set America Free.* New York: Bloomsbury Press, 2011.

Jim Dick

There have been many books published dealing with the causes and events that led to why the American colonies declared their independence from Great Britain. Many people often think it was inevitable that America declared its independence when in truth it was anything but that. There is ample evidence that a large group of people throughout the colonies and even in the Second Continental Congress that were in favor of reconciliation with Great Britain even as late as May 1776. The battles within Independence Hall between those that favored reconciliation and independence are not so well known, and that story is just as important to the early years of the Revolutionary era as those of Lexington and Concord, Bunker Hill, and the siege of Boston.

John Ferling tells the story of how the interests of the colonies and their delegates to Congress changed from reconciliation to independence. He also illustrates the anxiety the issue of independence caused for the Americans before they made the fateful leap of faith from being colonies of the British Empire to states of a new nation. Ferling, a professor emeritus of history at the University of West Georgia uses his extensive knowledge of the Revolutionary period to great effect in *Independence.* His use of biographical vignettes explaining the delegate's view on the issues at hand is a masterful stroke, which keeps the reader engrossed in the narrative. When coupled with the small details, he shows the delegates as men who reached their final decision over months of deliberation, not as a kneejerk reaction.

Ferling describes the struggle of those who favored independence versus those favoring reconciliation as an ongoing debate that was heavily dependent upon events outside Philadelphia. *Independence* reveals that the decisions were anything but inevitable until both the common people and their representatives reached the same conclusion regarding their futures. By placing the struggle as that between men and their ideas and interests, he removes it from a series of events to that of how the personal interaction of the delegates was just as important to the process. The end result is a book that adds to our understanding of how those men came to the decisions they reached when they cast the fateful vote on July 2, 1776.

Stephen Saunders Webb, *1676: The End of American Independence*, New York: Syracuse University Press, 1995.

Shawn Ryan

Stephen Saunders Webb informs readers that he was driven to write this book because, "the tale of 1676 is worth the telling," and his goal was to "pay tribute" to the people of this time for they shaped the American future. This three volume series explores different perspectives of the titled year 1676. The first and longest book in his volume of work is *Bacon's Revolution*; Webb offers substantial information on the revolt along with background information on Nathaniel Bacon and William Berkeley. Furthermore, he introduces lesser-known figures that aid in the explanations of events that in combination led to tragedy and the reshaping of Colonial America. The second and shortest book, *The World Viewed from Whitehall*, analyzes the events of 1676 from the British government's perspective. It contains a side to the story that is not as well-known, and provides the reader with an understanding of the connections between colonists and the monarchy. The last book, *The Anglo-Iroquoian Empire*, introduces Native American's role in this saga of 1676. This book emphasizes the Five Nations' relationship with the French and English and serves a secondary function as a partial biography for Garacontié. Without the inclusion of Garacontié, Webb's purpose would fall short since his conversion to Catholicism was crucial to negotiations.

Webb uncovers many connections and angles, but he forces too much information leaving the reader overwhelmed and needing to revisit certain areas for clarity. What Webb lacks in fluid writing, he more than makes up in other areas. The primary benefit is the extensive information in a single collection and serves as the best source for 1676. Each book contains a section titled "Some Suggested Reading." These help the reader understand the sources used and offer additional reading. The "Conclusions" section has improved readability and it is phenomenal at summarizing Webb's arguments. Included also are illustrations and maps with an entire section dedicated to the history surrounding them. Stephen Saunders Webb took on an immensely daunting task in preparing his book *1676: The End of American Independence*. He clearly presents an argument, indispensable for those scholars seeking detailed attributes of Colonial America in the year 1676 that shows how these events affected the future of America.

124

Johan Huizinga, *The Autumn of the Middle Ages*. Translated by Rodney J. Payton and Ulrich Mammitzsch. Chicago: University of Chicago Press, 1996.

Anne Midgley

Johan Huizinga's cultural history classic *Herfsttij der Middeleeuwen: Studie over levens- en gedachtenvormen der veertiende en vijftiende eeuw in Frankrijk en de Nederlanden* can be puzzling for English-speaking readers. Originally written in Dutch, the book itself has had a long history, having been continuously published since 1921, written in sixteen languages, and available in over 300 editions. Initially, *Herfsttij* received a mixed reception, but has since been regarded as a masterpiece of literature as well as a significant historical work.

Huizinga, seen by many as the greatest Dutch historian of the twentieth century, wrote during the period considered to be the age of classic cultural history. In many ways similar to his predecessor, Jacob Burckhardt, Huizinga sought to recover the soul of the time period he studied; in Huizinga's case, the late Middle Ages. Huizinga argued that the culture of the fourteenth and fifteenth centuries in France and the Netherlands was not the beginning of the Renaissance, but rather, that it represented the overly ripened fruits of the Middle Ages.[1] He defines much that has been attributed to the Renaissance to in fact be characteristic of the medieval period. Huizinga's examples include an analysis of the work of Jan van Eyck, concluding that van Eyck's art, while often regarded as "announcing the arrival of the Renaissance, should rather be regarded as the complete unfolding of the medieval spirit."[2]

Huizinga's prose immerses the reader in the fourteenth and fifteenth centuries of northern Europe. He draws upon the works of the chroniclers of the age, most frequently Jean Froissart, Olivier de la Marche, Georges Chastellain, and Enguerrand de Monstrelet, as well as the theologians, Denis the Carthusian and Jean De Gerson, the poet, Eustache Deschamps, and artists, primarily van Eyck. He paints a world vastly different than that of the early twentieth century with his opening "When the world was half a thousand years younger all events had much sharper outlines . . . all things in life had about them something glitteringly and cruelly public."[3] Huizinga is at his strongest as he builds sights, sounds, smells, color, and emotion into the portrait he paints of the age. The reader is swept away.

While the Payton and Mammitzsch translation seeks to bring *Herfsttij* closer to English readers, it misses an opportunity to provide modern readers with a better appreciation of the period through the use of color plates to portray the art works described in the text. The choice to rely on black and white plates is especially disappointing when one compares color to black and white representations of Jan van Eyck's *Annunciation*. The colors glow and shimmer in a color rendition of the painting; small details abound that are not apparent in black and white. Given Huizinga's desire that his readers experience as much as possible the life of the period, it is unfortunate that the new edition did not offer at least a few color plates of the many art works described in the text.[4]

Regardless of its faults, *Autumn* has aged extremely well; unlike many other ninety year old books, much of it remains fresh and powerful. *Autumn* is a true classic and its author, Johan Huizinga, continues long after his death to wield a strong influence, particularly for cultural historians.

Notes

1. Peter Burke, *What is Cultural History* (Cambridge: Polity, 2008), 7-10; Huizinga, *Autumn*, xix.

2. Huizinga, *Autumn*, 319.

3. Huizinga, *Autumn*, 1.

4. Huizinga, *Autumn*, plate 29; Jan van Eyck, *The Annunciation,* National Gallery of Art, Washington DC, http://www.artbible.info/art/large/505.html (accessed May 31, 2011).

Anglo-Saxon Hoard: Gold from England's Dark Ages

National Geographic Museum, Washington, D.C.

Candace McGovern

Currently on exhibit at the National Geographic Museum, the Anglo-Saxon Hoard provides a brief but thorough examination of a large hoard found in Staffordshire, England. The museum does an outstanding job presenting the largest collection of Anglo-Saxon gold ever found, valued at close to $5 million dollars. Since the majority of artifacts are military in style, the exhibition also includes an in-depth analysis of Mercia, a powerful Anglo-Saxon kingdom, known for their aggressiveness.

Beginning with a section detailing the contents and history of the hoard, visitors unfamiliar with the time period and terminology are welcome to read large texts covering a range of topics introduced in the exhibition. In the main room, curators divided artifacts by type with a particular emphasis on military and religious objects. Since the majority of artifacts are small, it is difficult for an untrained eye to determine the purpose of many objects. To overcome this, the museum has incorporated computer displays, which allow the visitor to zoom in on different objects and determine their functionality. This incorporation of technology serves only to enhance the visitor's knowledge. Aside from military artifacts such as pummels and other sword parts, other cases focus on the clergy with golden crosses and jewelry. Short videos stationed throughout the exhibit also enhance the visitor's experience and explain a variety of topics ranging from "how English craftsmen fashioned gemstones to the gold objects" to a video on "the history of the hoard," which includes theories of who buried it and how it was discovered. The second wing provides a less scholarly approach to the period and shifts to everyday life during the "Dark Ages." Aimed at children, this section covers clothing along with the language used in England at the time. The hands-on section for children allows them a chance to operate a metal detector and hunt for buried objects.

The scholarship behind the exhibition is, as expected from National Geographic, outstanding. The curators walk visitors through the process of rural excavation in England by incorporating video reenactments. Whenever possible, curators used actual objects for displays, particularly pummels from sword

127

handles. Aside from simply presenting a find, the exhibition includes important background information allowing anyone to walk away feeling like they have attended a seminar on the topic. Overall, this is an outstanding exhibition and historians and archaeologists or the public should not miss it.

Editor's note: The exhibit ran from October 29, 2011 to March 4, 2012.

Featured Titles from Westphalia Press

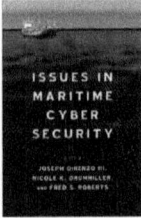

Issues in Maritime Cyber Security Edited by Nicole K. Drumhiller, Fred S. Roberts, Joseph DiRenzo III and Fred S. Roberts

While there is literature about the maritime transportation system, and about cyber security, to date there is very little literature on this converging area. This pioneering book is beneficial to a variety of audiences looking at risk analysis, national security, cyber threats, or maritime policy.

The Death Penalty in the Caribbean: Perspectives from the Police Edited by Wendell C. Wallace PhD

Two controversial topics, policing and the death penalty, are skillfully interwoven into one book in order to respond to this lacuna in the region. The book carries you through a disparate range of emotions, thoughts, frustrations, successes and views as espoused by police leaders throughout the Caribbean

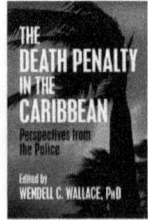

Middle East Reviews: Second Edition Edited by Mohammed M. Aman PhD and Mary Jo Aman MLIS

The book brings together reviews of books published on the Middle East and North Africa. It is a valuable addition to Middle East literature, and will provide an informative read for experts and non-experts on the MENA countries.

Unworkable Conservatism: Small Government, Freemarkets, and Impracticality by Max J. Skidmore

Unworkable Conservatism looks at what passes these days for "conservative" principles—small government, low taxes, minimal regulation—and demonstrates that they are not feasible under modern conditions.

The Politics of Impeachment Edited by Margaret Tseng

This edited volume addresses the increased political nature of impeachment. It is meant to be a wide overview of impeachment on the federal and state level, including: the politics of bringing impeachment articles forward, the politicized impeachment proceedings, the political nature of how one conducts oneself during the proceedings and the political fallout afterwards.

Demand the Impossible: Essays in History as Activism
Edited by Nathan Wuertenberg and William Horne

Demand the Impossible asks scholars what they can do to help solve present-day crises. The twelve essays in this volume draw inspiration from present-day activists. They examine the role of history in shaping ongoing debates over monuments, racism, clean energy, health care, poverty, and the Democratic Party.

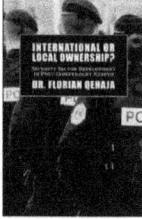

International or Local Ownership?: Security Sector Development in Post-Independent Kosovo
by Dr. Florian Qehaja

International or Local Ownership? contributes to the debate on the concept of local ownership in post-conflict settings, and discussions on international relations, peacebuilding, security and development studies.

Donald J. Trump's Presidency: International Perspectives
Edited by John Dixon and Max J. Skidmore

President Donald J. Trump's foreign policy rhetoric and actions become more understandable by reference to his personality traits, his worldview, and his view of the world. As such, his foreign policy emphasis was on American isolationism and economic nationalism.

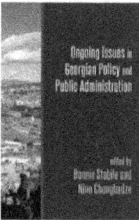

Ongoing Issues in Georgian Policy and Public Administration
Edited by Bonnie Stabile and Nino Ghonghadze

Thriving democracy and representative government depend upon a well functioning civil service, rich civic life and economic success. Georgia has been considered a top performer among countries in South Eastern Europe seeking to establish themselves in the post-Soviet era.

Poverty in America: Urban and Rural Inequality and Deprivation in the 21st Century
Edited by Max J. Skidmore

Poverty in America too often goes unnoticed, and disregarded. This perhaps results from America's general level of prosperity along with a fairly widespread notion that conditions inevitably are better in the USA than elsewhere. Political rhetoric frequently enforces such an erroneous notion.

westphaliapress.org